I0160048

When All Hell
Breaks Loose

How to Weather the

Storms of Life

by

LaVender Shedrick Williams &

Artist Deborah A. Shedrick

© 2016 Candy Publishing, LLC

All rights reserved. No part of this book may be reproduced, stored in a retrieval system or transmitted in any form or by any means, electronic or mechanical, including photocopying, recording, or by any information storage and retrieval system without the prior written permission of the publisher.

All artwork is copyrighted and may not be copied or duplicated without permission from the artist, Deborah A. Shedrick.

ISBN: 978-0-692-64290-0

Published by Candy Publishing, LLC

Printed in the United States

Editor
Jackie D. Rockwell

Contributing Writers

Alicia Hobdy
Aundria Long Jackson
Laura Kirk
Carys Kirk
Tori W. W. McCollum
Barbara J. Stokes

When All Hell
Breaks Loose

CONTENTS

Covered

I can only write about what I know; and I know a little somethin' somethin' about storms. I'm not speaking of rain storms, tropical storms, snow storms, or hurricanes, but it's the spiritual storms I'm most familiar with. I've experienced my share of storms, and even a Category IV Hurricane, but they didn't touch me or get my attention like the spiritual storms I've endured.

You're familiar with spiritual storms aren't you? You know those troublesome and trying times that attempt to make you lose your religion or make you look like you never had any religion to begin with. What about a challenging time in your life when you didn't know up from down. Have you ever been involved in a relationship that made you feel like you were losing your mind? What about a situation that pushed you to the edge and revealed a part of your character you never met? Those situations are what we call storms – hardships, difficult times, or life issues having the capability to touch every aspect of our life.

In the midst of what I categorize as a tropical storm designed to destroy my life, was actually the beginning of one of the most beautiful seasons of my life. Not only did the very intense seemingly destructive storm force me to step out of my comfort zone and place of financial security, but this storm brought a wind system that stirred gifts that were sitting dormant in my spirit for years. This storm was the blaster that forced me to get up and move from a place I said I'd never leave. The storm showed me courage I didn't know I had. It forced me to look fear in the face without blinking. **This** storm introduced me to a God I'd never met.

Just when I thought that storm was over and it was safe to go outside, I got comfortable. But then another storm came and almost knocked me off my feet, again. I wasn't expecting back to back storms. But these storms came, and they came quickly with little time to prepare. I thought I knew peace, but this second storm, on top of that first one, introduced me to some peace that surpassed all human understanding. I thought I knew joy, but this one showed me unspeakable joy. I thought I had life, but, I am convinced in the aftermath, that the intense pressure and hurricane force winds of these storms showed me how to live my life, and live it more abundantly.

The storms that made my life appear like it was falling apart were actually making things fall into place. As the storm arranged some things and rearranged others, I was evolving into the woman I always envisioned myself to be. I was becoming the woman God created me to be, but was afraid to be: An independent, courageous, outspoken, fearless woman who embraced every minute of life and lived with no regrets - a woman who enjoyed her own company without apologies - a woman who didn't mind being a little selfish to renew her mind, body, and soul - a woman experiencing guilt-free happiness. A storm surge came and attempted to destroy me; and when it was all over, I found the new me ashore and spiritually awake.

I fought these storms for so long and resisted having to endure them. It tossed and turned my life upside down. The storm emptied me of everything I had except the two sons I gave birth to. The storm placed me in a position to be used in a way I never thought possible. I had to be stripped, bruised, and broken in order to be spiritually enlightened and blessed beyond my wildest imagination. I was freed from a paralyzing bondage that almost succeeded at preventing me from seeing clearly.

As Johnny Nash says in his classic hit song, *I can see clearly now the rain has gone. I can see all obstacles in my way. Gone are the dark clouds that had me blind. I think I can make it now the pain is gone. All the bad feelings have disappeared. There is that rainbow I've been praying for. It's gonna be a bright, bright, sun-shiny day.*

Unfortunately, I wasn't able to sing that song while going *through* the storm. I had to see a glimpse of the rainbow first. I felt like my merciful God had forsaken me. I felt lost and alone, but the Holy Spirit found a way through my thick layer of doubts and fears to deliver words of peace and comfort. He whispered softly, "I'm here; trust Me. I've got you covered."

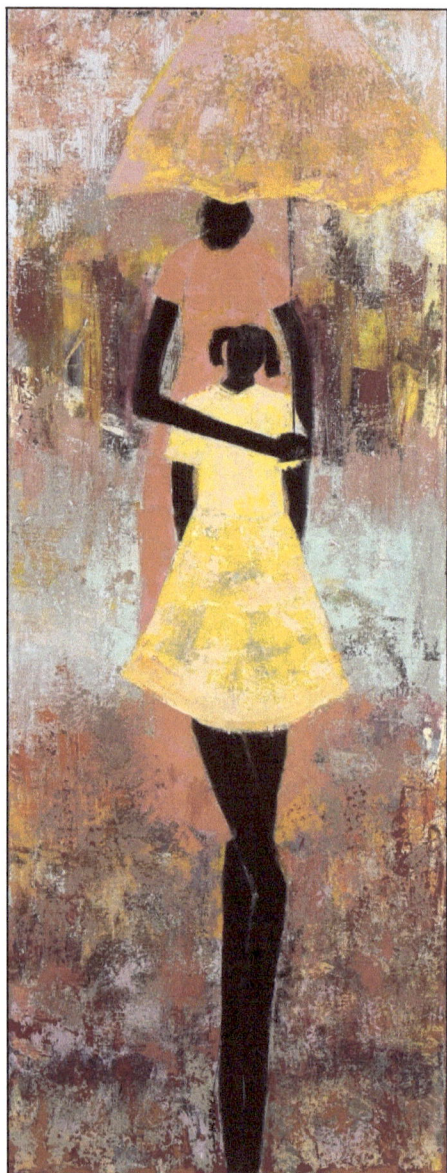

For Women Only

Why a survival guide exclusively for women? Well, I refuse to act like I know how a man thinks – especially when they go through storms. Men have too much doggone ego to sift through, for me to begin to understand what they're thinking. Also, some of them lack the ability to communicate what they feel and be truthful about it. So it's safe for me to just stick with writing what I know, and I know women.

I know the heart of a woman and how we try to keep it together when storms of life hit our heart and our home. Let's face it, a woman is the super glue that keeps family, friendships, and all those other relationships together, yet we often come unglued in the eye of a storm that our spiritual eyes didn't see forming on the horizon. It's always easier to forecast a storm in someone else's life quicker than in our own. As women, we often see the barely visible rainbow at the end of another's storm before we recognize the one promised to us. We offer powerful words of encouragement and prayer to others going through something, yet struggle to edify ourselves.

On top of being the glue to hold everything and everyone else together, women deal with internal issues that haunt us and attempt to control and influence our reactions to external circumstances. Changing hormones, moods, chemical imbalances in the brain and body, PMS, peri-menopause, and menopause, are just a few internal issues we deal with; I'm sure there are a few more. These reoccurring issues *can* be controlled, yet as busy women, taking care of our body is not always a priority, and these internal issues are given the power to control us instead of us controlling them. Throughout this book, I will refer to *Ms. Flesh* – the ugly part of me. Ms. Flesh usually surfaces when I've neglected my mind, body, and spirit. I blame the actions I'm not so proud of on her. You have a Ms. Flesh too, and I'm sure you have daily battles with her just as I do.

A woman's health and mental state play a great part in our performance in a storm. Our physical body influences our mental reaction. In other words, the body follows the mind. So, instead of snapping over insignificant matters, we can maintain a better poise of spiritual balance when we make exercising and healthy eating a habit – a lifestyle. When we feel better, we act better. I'm a witness.

I'm wired as a high strung individual. My daily prayer is that the Spirit of God will hide me from myself and consume me with His Spirit because this sister - can go off! I like to blame it on hormones. My younger sister lovingly reminds me that I'm not fit for society during a special time of the month. I laugh about it, but sadly her statement is true because I don't want to own that ugly part of me - Ms Flesh. We don't always see or hear ourselves for who we really are. I've also been called *bossy* by a close friend. I could easily blame this on my twenty-year military career, but uh…it's all me. I'm not afraid to admit and own who I am, but the last thing I need when going through a storm, is a bad attitude or an ugly disposition to make me act and react like a crazy woman out of control. Sit down somewhere, Ms. Flesh!

I notice a significant difference in my attitude when I put healthy foods in my body. I love my desserts, but sugar invites Ms. Flesh to appear and have her way. When I return to loving my body and making it a priority, I also return to my mental place of peace – a place of agreement with the Spirit of God and clear thinking. Some women are on the verge of divorce once a month not realizing the problem may be within themselves. We'll cry over spilled milk one day, and the next day spill more milk without reacting at all. It's not the milk! I learned to love myself *and* my life enough to take better care of me. Don't wait until you get sick to take care of yourself. Make your temple a priority every waking day. Show God gratitude for your life by taking care of it. It may be hard to admit, but some of us provide better preventive maintenance on our cars more than we provide temple maintenance.

I recall a project a few women and I were working on years ago. We functioned on fumes and adrenalin from beginning to end, and there was no time to rest. The project was a success and we received endless compliments, yet the laborious work took a toll on us. My older sister and I talked about how some women live this type of strenuous lifestyle, week after week. This may be the reason heart disease is the number one killer of women. A lifestyle of constant busyness invites mental stress.

Our minds say keep going, but our bodies beg us to stop and renew. We listen to our mind but think we are so important, that we must keep going. Trust me, if we die, we *will* be replaced. If I can be real, we don't even have to die to be replaced. It may appear glamorous, and some women feel validated having such a full schedule, but why?

What we do doesn't define us. While scheduling events and appointments, consider scheduling a day to renew your mind and body. Every day of the week doesn't have to be filled with errands and projects.

"My mission in life is not merely to survive, but to thrive;
and to do so with some passion, some compassion, some
humor, and some style."

Maya Angelou

Hell Broke Loose

The mission of this survival guide is to share what I've learned through my own spiritual storms with hopes of helping other storm walkers. I've made some unwise choices and embarrassed my Heavenly Father more than a few times, but prayerfully my experiences and life lessons will offer enlightenment and encouragement to the forecasted storms in your life. They are definitely coming!

As I allow you to look into my life and learn from it, courtesy of my personal storms, please know I do not have it perfectly altogether. With each storm came the profound lesson of sharing myself while riding out the storm. I am now fully aware that the power is *in* the storm. We often make the mistake of being quiet and fading in the crowd when a storm hits. We get to ourselves and wait for the storm to pass and then shout, "He brought me through!" Uh...brought you through what? We bask in God's glory, but very few want to tell their story. I've been guilty of this, as well.

Let it be known that I only learned my lessons when hell broke loose in my life, and unfortunately, just like those storms, hell breaking loose was not a one-time event. Some storms of my life have had a greater impact than others. I've thrived through some, and felt like I barely survived the others. Some storms seemed like rain showers while others felt like hail storms, pelting me in mid flight, forcing a painful landing. There were storms where I felt like more than a conqueror, while others I felt like the weakest link.

It's ironic, but some storms I don't even remember, while others left scars to purposely remind me of what I went through.

Trust me when I say, I would not be in a position to share unless I've gone through my own storms. Storms aren't to gloat and beam about when we come out of them, but to reach back and help someone else going through. We often forget this important part when our storm issue is in remission. When I began writing this book, I hadn't intended on sharing my own storms, yet what good is it to say, "I made it through" without sharing *what* I came through.

We all have a testimony, but are we willing to share the specific test? Storms can be embarrassing to share, but I'm always reminded that my life is not my own. The embarrassing part is probably because we've unwittingly created a false persona that says we don't have troubles. Happy face equals happy family, happy marriage, happy finances, happy career. Right? Wrong. Happy often means I'm going through, but I'm alright. I'm bruised and I've been broken, but God made my jagged edges smooth again. I've been through the fire, but I remain faithful. Church women are notorious for the happy face, and although we don't have to look like what we've been through, when the opportunity presents itself, and we're asked, let's consider sharing our storm with another storm walker. Once we share, others won't feel so alone and isolated through their storm. It takes an enormous amount of courage and compassion to allow our life to become a mirror for others. Remember, we're sharing to reveal the glory of God...not ourselves.

"We are troubled on every side, yet not distressed; we are perplexed, but not in despair; persecuted, but not forsaken; cast down, but not destroyed…"

II Corinthians 4:8,9

Looking back over the aftermath of our weakened storms helps prepare for future storms and also helps others who may be going through similar storms. It's a blessing to be used while in the midst of a storm, but it takes courage to admit being in a storm. Again, we like to appear to be perfectly packaged with our makeup and stilettos, when behind the makeup is distress, and we're about to fall in those heels.

I understand more than ever that God *is* in control of each storm, from the beginning stages to that glorious time when the storm dissipates and calm is restored. I believe each storm that comes my way is allowed and divinely designed for me. I believe I am covered – like a blanket stitched with my Heavenly Father's love and protection.

Prepare for the Storm

Living in Florida has taught me how to prepare for hurricanes. Fortunately, there are weather forecasters to forewarn residents when a tropical storm is stirring and the possibility of it turning into a hurricane. As the storm travels inland, the time to prepare also draws nearer. Gas lines are longer, water and can goods disappear from grocery store shelves, and windows are boarded. If you're smart, you won't wait until the last minute to prepare, but you'll beat the lines and keep a stock of necessary items on hand.

Timing is essential. If you're paying attention you won't have to hustle along with everybody else, because you'll be ready. After your calm (or intense) preparation, the waiting period begins. You've got everything you need and you know where your people are. With eyes glued to the television and ears on the radio, we pray the predictions won't come true.

A spiritual storm should be prepared for in the same way regardless of the nature of the storm. Unfortunately, we can't always tell the direction the storm will come, but we know it's coming. The storm can be financial, marital, mental, family, health, or a soul storm, which is, in my opinion, the most difficult storm to prepare for. Soul storms are those storms dealing with our emotions. You know, those storms dealing with relationships that cut to the core of the heart and sometimes cutting it in half.

Unlike severe weather storms, instead of stock piling bottled water, filling up on gas, and boarding windows, spiritual storms require preparation of the spiritual mind and a donning of the armor – the whole armor of God. It will fit you and serve you well, to be strong in the Lord and His mighty power. The secret to preparation for spiritual storms is to *always* be prepared – don't wait for the storm to hit. If you wait, it's almost a guarantee you'll be part of the madness of and calling on scripture to tame those thoughts of doubt, fear, and confusion, instead of speaking to one another in psalms and songs and hymns of thanksgiving.

Women, use your intuition. It's our greatest tool in life. That feeling that "something isn't right" is a feeling we know, yet don't always acknowledge. We brush it off, ignore it, or think it's "just a feeling." Well that "feeling" is a powerful GPS to guide us in life as a woman, wife, and mother. That "feeling" is God's gift to us. That "feeling" prepares our hearts and minds for what's ahead of us that we cannot see. That "feeling" can only be tapped into when we tap into the One who gave it to us. When we abide in Him, He abides in us. When it's already on, use it. When you need to turn it on, do it. In other words we must stick to, stay connected to, conform to, adhere to, and follow Him in order to recognize and acknowledge "the feeling."

It's easy for me to abide by staying in tune to the Holy Spirit. Staying in tune means I mentally stay in a place to hear His voice. When I stay in tune, I know I'm abiding. Staying in tune assures me I'm on the right track. I don't have to wonder if the voice I hear is Him, me, or the enemy within me, which I create from my own doubts and fears. Staying in tune to the Spirit doesn't allow the many voices in life to distract me from spiritual guidance (GPS). Abiding is crucial preparation for imminent storms.

Abiding is a process and takes intimate time in prayer (talking) and even more time in meditation (listening). I am strengthened in times of solitude, so consecrated, contemplated time in prayer is a must for me, but one prayer in the morning doesn't cut it for me. There are too many things and too many people to deal with in the course of my day to depend on one prayer. I had to develop a praying spirit. I learned to pray without ceasing. This doesn't mean my lips are always moving, but spending daily, quality time with God allows my mind to be consumed more with the Spirit of God than Ms. Flesh – that ugly part of me that enjoys showing up during a good storm.

Ms. Flesh still shows up uninvited, but I'm more aware of her presence now. I know how to silence her and put her in her place, but she is definitely strong-willed and wants to have her way. I admit I've allowed Ms. Flesh to have her way on numerous occasions and actually felt good about it, but later felt a pang of guilt – I know better.

Ms. Flesh never shows up alone. She travels with friends named distractions. Those distractions come in countless shapes and forms. The very things God blesses me with, Ms. Flesh finds a way to turn it into a distraction, which only gets in the way of my fellowship with God. A job, house, husband, significant other, friend, children, to-do list, unfinished tasks, dreams, cell phone, television, school, cell phone, vision boards, goals, cars, bills, hobbies, food, new endeavors, cell phone, ipad, ipod, laptop, money, needs, issues, or anything can become a distraction and hinder abiding. I can't name them all. We share some of the same distractions and some we create ourselves. Do you know what your distractions are?

Meditation is the key for me. Distractions disappear when we take time to be quiet. If I can be real, sometimes we have to learn when to sit down and shut up. We have to learn to stop being so busy or acting like we're busy, and stop acting like everything we've got going on is so important. Learning to be still in the presence of God is one of the most valuable lessons I've learned, and the most helpful during a storm.

Meditation can be difficult because the mind tends to wander. One minute you're meditating and the next minute you're thinking about what to cook for dinner, or what happened at work yesterday. I'm not excused from the wandering mind, but I find focusing on each breath helps me remain focused. Being aware of each inhale and exhale quiets my busy mind. Every breath is a blessing, yet we aren't always aware of it because we take it for granted. Stop and take a few minutes to notice the blessing of breathing - life! You can do that right now: Stop. Inhale. Hold it. Think about it. Thank God for it. Exhale. Think about it. Thank God for it. That's meditation! Life!

We never know what the day will bring – or the season. I remember the spring of 2015. It was *supposed* to be spring, but there was snow, ice, heat, and rain from coast to coast. Each state was experiencing their "spring" season, and my city, Pensacola, was experiencing all four seasons in one day. The funny thing is how we expected spring to invite warm weather. Of course, it usually does, but Mother Nature showed us that she can do what she wants, when she wants, and how she wants. Mother Nature can also change her mind mid-day without explanation. Again, the key is to be prepared. That particular spring season reminded me of the seasons of life. As life changes, we have to be like the wind and go with the flow.

Weather is unpredictable and so is life. So unless we learn to adapt and adjust, we'll live a miserable and frustrated life. Father Time and Mother Nature work together, and our only job in their process is to be content in whatever season of life we find ourselves in. Yes, the calendar may say it's spring, yet someone is going through a storm while someone else may be experiencing the happiest day of their life. Someone somewhere is grieving, someone is sick, someone's health has been restored, someone is being born, and someone took their last breath last night. Life happens, and the best way to enjoy it is to not expect a sunny day every day, and be prepared for whatever the day brings, and stay covered -just in case. You've probably heard the phrase – You're either in a storm, coming out of a storm, or about to enter a storm; and only God knows how hard it'll hit. It's called LIFE.

The rain is needed on Earth *and* in our lives. We sometimes complain about the rain, but without the rain there is no rainbow. It all works together. White light enters one individual rain droplet and exits as one specific color of the spectrum. Without millions of rain droplets, a rainbow would not occur. If we only had a few rain droplets, we would only see a few colors. This is typically why rainbows appear after a rain storm.

There will always be challenges, mountains to climb, valleys to walk through, upsets to endure and tribulations to try our faith and our character. Life has a way of teaching lessons regardless if we've registered for the class or not. Life *will* have its way. The spring of 2015 may not have made any sense to us, but it made perfect sense to the One who created it.

It was 2:30 a.m. one morning, and I was wide awake. My mind was racing with thoughts of life, so I decided to write a little. I prayed, meditated and even watched a few minutes of a Netflix movie, but I couldn't fall asleep. I've always said when one wakes up in the middle of the night, it's the time to listen to God. He doesn't have to compete with my busyness and the voices in my ear. He has my undivided attention. The last time I went through one of these early morning wake-ups, I later found out the Lord was preparing me to be prayed up. This is how I know that being in tune and recognizing "that feeling" works.

As much as I wished my early morning wake-ups were connected to menopausal insomnia, I didn't want to take a chance. I chose to be prayed up and prepared, so I spent time in prayer. After praying, I listened. God's presence is amazingly humbling and awe-inspiring, so if you've never experienced it, you're in for an awakening – no pun intended. The thought that God loves me enough to prepare me for what's ahead of me is mind-blowing. The fact that He ushers me into His presence in the wee hours of the morning is breath-taking. Don't take it lightly when God gets your attention. He loves us and wants nothing but the best for His daughters and He'll take us through whatever category storm necessary to bless us. Is God preparing you?

Perception of the Storm

Since we know God's covering is our strength to walk through the storms of life, why do we sometimes find ourselves mentally losing it when a storm approaches? Why do we fret and try to immediately escape the storm or make it disappear? Do you shake your head in disgust or frustration because of the timing of the storm? Do you hang your head, curse, take your anger out on someone else, sulk, eat, or find a way to be alone in your feelings? Have you ever said, "The devil is a lie. I rebuke this in the name of Jesus." Or maybe you've said, "I'm not claiming this." News flash! It doesn't matter if you claim it or not. God is God and we don't have any power or authority to rebuke a storm He sends.

God doesn't sit around and design storms to simply deliver us from it because we ask. Well, He can, but what are we learning by asking for deliverance from a storm? Just as quickly as we run away from one storm, we'll run right into the same storm sooner or later. For those of you who aren't afraid to admit you sometimes unravel at the edges when storms arise, continue reading. For those who've never unraveled, you're an exception to this section of the book because you obviously have the spiritually correct perception of storms when they hit. Congratulations, Sister Saint!

Would it be safe to say that the severity of a storm is a factor in how we react to it? I'm not so sure because one person's storm may not cause another person to react at all, but the bottom line is – we all will endure storms on different levels. Whether it's a storm regarding a difficult co-worker, a storm dealing with a troubled teenager, a toddler in temper tantrum season, a needy adult child, a controlling husband, or limited finances, we all endure storms on some level. We're all wired differently, so be careful not to minimize one's mountain that appears to be a molehill to you. Different storms push different buttons.

Our coping skills vary, and some may have never developed any coping skills at all. I was once the woman who became unglued during a storm, and desperately searched for a listening ear. I came to the conclusion that after talking about the storm so much, no one *really* gave a damn and was dealing with their own storms. I quickly learned to step back, take a breath, and think before I acted like a woman who had lost her mind. I'm more than thankful for my sisters and a friend or two who will listen to my mumbling, grumbling and complaining without judging me. Well, one friend actually told me I complain a lot. You know who you are and I thank you - I think. Have you encountered a storm with the potential to push you to the end of your rope? Hold on. The storm is coming, but we are already fully equipped to endure. As my grandmother and so many other wise women have said, "Keep on livin'."

On the other hand, there are some storm walkers who think they know it all and can solve their storm issues and yours too. They belittle the fact you're in a storm and that you're worried about your issue. As far as they're concerned, you caused your storm because of your inability to make wise decisions. They walk with their head high knowing good and well their own life is not a bed of roses, but want everyone to think they've got it all together. So they Bible tote and scripture quote every time they open their mouth. As my grandmother and so many other wise women have said, "Keep on livin'."

Our perception of a storm is crucial to our reaction to the storm. Let me say it this way – how we perceive the storm determines how we perform through the storm. For some reason, it's easier to always think the worse of any situation. If we're sick, we think we might have cancer. If our teenage daughter is always tired, we think she might be pregnant. If our husband is late getting home, he's with another woman. Our thoughts seem to automatically go to the worst places without much effort on our part, but being aware of those initial thoughts can help us change our way of thinking. I'm here to tell you, we <u>can</u> tame our carnal thoughts and direct them to be more positive, more spiritual. Being spiritually minded affirms us that *whatever* the situation is, it has GOT to be working for our good – if we believe. Being spiritually minded reminds us that it's *already* alright – if we believe. Being spiritually minded reminds us that God is in control – if we believe.

"Even the worst thing that has ever happened to you happened for your good."

Dr. Timothy J. Winters, Bayview Baptist Church
San Diego, CA

It can be difficult to even imagine a crisis working for our good. If we think logically, of course it doesn't appear to be for our good and it doesn't make any sense at all, but the spiritual mind works beyond the realm of logic. The spiritual mind leaves no room for debate on the storm working for our good. Even if the 'good' is something as simple as acknowledging our worth or value, it's good. A personal who has not received Christ may not understand this concept and it might sound foolish. Only the spiritual mind is capable of receiving words from the Spirit. This doesn't mean that just because you go to church, you're spiritually minded.

I remember the morning of the funeral of my aunt in Cleveland. While trying to be a source of comfort to my father, I received a phone call from my husband in Florida with the bad news that his son (my stepson) had died. Shocked, I asked him several times to repeat what he was saying, because surely he wasn't saying what I thought I was hearing. There I was, preparing to attend one funeral and hearing there would be another one. My stepson, in his early twenties, suddenly passed away in his sleep. How was this unbelievable time working for my good? My immediate thoughts did not at all process this situation in a spiritually correct way. As far as I was concerned, there was nothing good about the two lost lives – nothing. But did I learn anything from the situation? I did.

Through that seemingly senseless and untimely storm, I realized there must be a bigger picture in the storm than what my carnal eyes could see. I was reminded that my ways and thoughts are not God's ways and thoughts, and any effort to figure it out would've been a complete waste of time and energy. As much as I wanted to resist and deny what was happening, I knew the only thing I could do was to embrace what God was doing and pray through my pain. To be honest, that was all I was capable of doing. While I wanted to have a personal pity party, I knew my husband and his ex-wife were in extreme pain of their own. I had to get out of my own emotions and remember there were others closer to the storm, dealing with the same emotions on completely different levels. Although I was touched by this storm, it wasn't all about me.

There was nothing I could do about that particular storm. The deaths happened and whether I wanted to accept them or not, I had to deal with them. I didn't have a choice in the storm, yet I had a choice in my perception of it. I had a choice to be either pissed or at peace. It was my reaction to the storm that allowed me to come to the point of accepting God's will to call those two family members home at that time. This is definitely a process and may take several storms to get to this point of perception. Creating a habit of spiritual perception helps to prepare for future storms.

We often associate "working for your good" as something *we* gain or benefit from, but it is possible that *our* good is solely to benefit someone else. We can be a conduit for another's good. We are called to be vessels, right? Everything is not about us. We're all connected in this universe. We can be so self-centered that we create a "why me" disposition thinking we're the only ones being touched by the storm. Sometimes we are taken through difficult situations and storms that have very little to do with us if anything at all. We are used to touch the lives of others another – regardless of the situation.

I say, "Have your way, Lord!" all the time and one day I realized what I was actually saying. Was I really willing to allow God to have His way with me? Not that God needs my permission to have His way with me, but I was making myself available to be used in whatever manner God chose. I was willing to be an empty vessel to be used by Him in any way He wanted. With this being said, I should be able to peacefully embrace any storm God chooses for me to walk through. Oooouch!

Purpose of the Storm

It's actually a waste of time to try to figure out why and how God works in our life. If we actually stopped to consider His incredible sovereignty, we'd stop even trying. Scripture reminds us His ways and thoughts are not ours (Isaiah 55:9). In our finite wisdom we can't begin to comprehend God's way of thinking - it's inconceivable.

Though we walk through storms blindly, we're often blessed with a small portion of enlightenment once they are over. Even when we *think* we know the reason for a storm, other reasons reveal themselves. I believe under God's permissive will these storms occur for several reasons. I can only share the lessons learned from my own storms, and allow **His divine purpose (for my life) to come to fruition**. I don't always agree with what God is doing in my life, but I've learned not to resist because there is always a bigger picture I can't see. Most of the things and people I've fought in my life turned out to be a blessing. It's not always about me. Ms. Flesh is good at resisting God's will, and this always makes the storm more difficult to endure.. .

After many years of being a home schooling mother and full time wife, I decided to look for a job. I looked everywhere and put in many applications. I didn't know if I was too old or if I had been out of the work force for too long, but I couldn't seem to find any work. Burger King wouldn't even hire me! I stopped looking, but got a hunch to check a particular website. There I learned a radio station (whose owner I happened to know) was looking for an administrative assistant. I immediately sent my resume, and was called in for an interview. I got the job and the owner said he was going to teach me how to run the radio station.

I was so excited; I had a job! But after a few weeks, I didn't think I'd be able to handle it. It was just too much and administrative assistant was hardly a fitting title for the work I was doing. This job was more difficult for me to learn than my job as an Air Traffic Controller in the Navy. There were so many moving parts to learn, I felt like I was losing my mind. Instead of me working the job, the job was working me! I cried, whined, and complained. Talk about a storm? I was going through a HAIL storm and it was painful. I approached my boss about not being the person for the job – he wasn't hearing it. The patience he had with me amazes me even as to this day, as I am *still* learning.

As it turns out, I believe this job was one of the best things that ever happened to me. It changed my life on so many levels. Truthfully, I would have never taken the job if I had known what it entailed; which is why the *real* job was hidden under an Administrative Assistant title. I thought God set me up, and He did. Royally. I'm blessed to sit in one of the most difficult positions I've ever had, but first I had to walk through a severe storm.

And little did I know, God was using that storm to prepare me for another one- a marital one. Five months after being on my new job, I found myself walking away from my twenty-year marriage. The job I felt so inadequate in, that I was trying so hard to leave, was actually placing me in a position to be able to support myself.

Another reason I believe storms occur in my life is to **get my attention**. Sometimes busyness makes a woman feel like she has a little power. Because we can multi-task and get a to-do list done in record time with few glitches, the Superwoman syndrome arrives. We feel good about our accomplishments and end our day preparing for the next conquest. But after a while of this cycle, the ground beneath us has to be shaken up a bit. We need a quick jolt to remind us of the source of our strength, energy and power.. We need God's covering not only during a storm, but when things are seemingly okay.

Unfortunately, we learn very little in happy times. We have to be shaken up a bit to remember just how much we need a Savior. Oh yea, we'll say, "Thank you, Jesus" in happy times, but when we're going through a storm, that same 'Thank you, Jesus' is a little more gut-wrenching. An attention-getting storm can come from any angle – an unexpected financial obligation, a call from our child's school, a health scare, or anything that will make us stop in our tracks. We often have to be made to stop since we won't stop on our own. We can be skinning and grinning one minute and the next minute our mouth is wide open wondering how we got in the center of the storm. Be prepared! Abide! Recognize "the feeling." Don't get caught up living life, be aware of the life in you.

We have to learn to depend on God every minute of the day, not just when we're going through a storm. Worship is supposed to be a lifestyle, not an emergency 'get me through the storm' session. It's through God's permissive will of storms that we see just how secure and connected we are to our God. Not only is our faith revealed, but our fellowship with God is also revealed...or unraveled.

My younger sister helped me with the third reason storms occur in my life, which is to **keep me grounded.** She reminded me that my spiritual roots were so strong and secure, she didn't have a doubt that I'd make it through a severe soul storm I was going through. She texted me in the midst of my storm - "My new saying for you is, 'But dem roots though!' It doesn't matter if a tree is damaged and not bearing any fruit...that tree can sit there for years looking like a dried up eyesore...but honey child...if dem roots are still alive in the ground that tree can still come back! I know your roots are ANCHORED in the Lord God

31

Almighty! HUMPH! You are and forever will be just fine. Child your Daddy died on a cross...Yes, He did! The ultimate sacrifice was made for you and you are forgiven, loved, cherished, protected, and SET APART! Hold your head up, waaaay up, and say to the enemy, "But dem roots though!"

Sometimes others know our strength better than we do. My sister definitely encouraged me, and reminded me that my soul was anchored and my roots were strong. My storms remind me of dem roots that keep me grounded. We forget the strength we have within us. I love it..."But dem roots though!"

If we don't have roots, we're in trouble. From early childhood through adulthood, I was rooted in the functions of the church. I've got enough preaching and Word in me that I should have no problem looking at a storm and saying, "Bring it on! I'm covered."

The final reason for storms in my life is a **test of my faithfulness**. Being faithful can be one of the most difficult things to do, and being faithful in a storm can be more difficult. We fail at faithfulness during storms mainly because of our impatience. We try to manipulate the storm, control it, or make it disappear through our own works instead of letting God work. Instead, we must surrender our will and allow God to have His way with us and through us in the storm. Will we trust God through the storm? Will we trust Him when our husband strays? Will we trust Him when we receive an unfavorable diagnosis? Will we trust Him when our children get off track? Will we trust Him with a negative bank account balance? Will we trust him when we receive a pink slip?

"Though He slay me, yet will I trust Him"

Job 13:15

A fellow mom and I have corresponded through email for years, and I've enjoyed reading about her daughters growing up and becoming young women. One of her daughters took a complete 180 degree turn in her life – away from the way she was raised. This sweet girl is now on drugs, in the streets, and making money however she can. What do you say to a mom whose heart is ripped and mind is confused? She only wanted her daughter back. I felt helpless. We all have our own journey in life, and so do our children.

The mother wanted the storm to immediately cease. She prayed her daughter would be delivered from the streets, yet the intensity of the storm seemed to increase. The mother did all she could do to rescue her daughter to no avail, and ended up having to sign away her rights to her daughter. It wasn't until the weary mother surrendered in this way, and stopped interfering with God's plan for her daughter that her baby girl eventually came home and asked for help. Her daughter needed to walk through her own storm and find her own way out.

It's difficult to sit and watch someone else go through a storm – especially our children. This Mama Bear is half crazy when it comes to her cubs, and I don't care how old they are. As they grow older and I grow spiritually, I'm learning to let go, but it isn't easy. I have a son in the Army and I find myself reassuring him that I'm here for him. However, I'm quickly reminded that not only do I have to trust the training I gave my son, but I have to trust God.

God controls our circumstances – we either believe this or we don't. Even if our circumstances fall apart right before our eyes, the faithful believer will recognize the situation has been strategically planned and perfectly timed. It's Divine Design. I often wonder if I make the Holy Spirit work overtime when I get in the way. In past storms, I would immediately try to figure out the dynamics of the storm and strategize a plan of attack. I knew there was a solution to the issue in my storm, but what I failed to realize is that it was already worked out – God didn't need my help. My job is to stop, drop and pray.

This is especially important when it comes to our friends and loved ones going through storms. Women like to vent, which can be therapeutic, but we also like to make things okay. The most valuable thing we can do for a friend is to get out of the way.

"...and when you begin to see that person in the middle of a difficult and painful struggle, don't try to prevent it, but pray that his difficulty will grow even ten times stronger until no power on earth or in hell could hold him away from Jesus Christ."

Oswald Chambers

The above quote is an excerpt from the devotional "My Utmost for His Highest." I shared it because it's the exact opposite of what I've done in the past when I saw someone dear to me going through a difficult storm. Women naturally like to act as caretakers in any situation. We want to fix things and make things better. It's hard watching someone go through a storm and we fear that if we don't step in, it will appear we don't care. Still, we have to be careful not to get in God's way by trying to be "amateur providences" in the lives of others.

I remember my mother saying, "If I could live your life for you, I would." I believe most mothers feel this way.. As women we feel called to protect our children, help our husbands, save our parents, and be the 'go-to' friend. But in reality we're hindering our loved ones from a closer walk with their *real* Helper. We must help and protect to a certain degree, and then we must allow God to be God. Sometimes I go overboard with my help. Mama can't always come to the rescue – although this mama tries to. My phrase is, "Call me if you need me!" Although difficult, I have learned to recognize the limitations of my earthly role, and make room for the magnitude of God's power. I remember my father asking me, "Why are you feeding the homeless? How do you know God isn't punishing him for something?" Daddy's statement sounds a little harsh and I don't know about the punishment part, but it's good to know when to step in and when to step out of someone else's storm.

What if we went through storms simply to suffer with Christ. What if the level of our mumbling, grumbling and complaining defined our level of love for God. What if?

Peace in the Storm

You may have wondered how you can have peace when your entire life is in turmoil. It's easy to tell someone to have peace – to be strong – stay prayerful, but while in the middle of a turbulent storm, their mind may not even be in a position to process what peace is. When a storm hits, the mind initially will have thoughts of doubt and fear unless we've maintained our spiritual connection and covering.

I remember having a discussion with a gentleman who found himself in a storm after making some unwise, selfish decisions. He mentioned he was going to start going to church more often. He was already a weekly church attendee, so I guess he meant he'd be in church every time the doors opened. Staying in church is fine, but staying covered and connected is better. What happens when the church doors are closed? What happens when the praise and worship music goes off? What happens when the preacher goes to sleep? You're left to endure the storm – alone. There is no one around to encourage you. No one is singing, preaching or offering prophetic words. All you have is yourself and your thoughts. This time alone will reveal your spiritual connection or lack thereof. Will your connection wires become frayed and unraveled or will they bear the never-ceasing flow of emotions and pressures from the storm? When the storm is raging, will you also rage or maintain poise through praise and prayer?

When a storm hits, it can knock you off your feet if you aren't able to quickly recall affirmations and scripture from memory. If you aren't able to encourage yourself, those damaging, untamed thoughts will invade your mind and consume your thoughts. If you have to scuffle for your Bible or your mediation book, you may find yourself quickly drowning. This is why it's important to stay prepared for storms by spending time in meditation with God.

This doesn't mean we have to walk around expecting something bad to happen but just by staying covered we can't be caught off guard. Storms may shake our ground, but we'll be able to stay spiritually minded. When those negative thoughts drop into your mind, hold them captive and don't allow them to get loose (2 Corinthians 10:5). Immediately replace those destructive thoughts of doubt with positive thoughts (Philippians 4:8). Remember, life guarantees storms – there is no escaping them.

Doesn't a good rainstorm or thunderstorm invite a good nap? I can sleep like a baby during a good thunderstorm. This thought comes to mind during spiritual storms. If I have the mind of a child and trust God through the storm, I should be able to sleep through it – peacefully. In other words, I shouldn't be shaken by the circumstances of the storm. I know God's got me covered and is working for my good – regardless of what the storm looks like. I don't need to lose sleep or walk the floors at night. Easier said than done? Of course it is, but it *can* be done.

"Why now?" This was a question a friend asked when a particular situation occurred in her life. She had a few things going on and wondered what was so special about 'right now' that God would allow a particular circumstance to change or unfold in her life. It wasn't a bad situation, it was actually a very exciting occurrence, but the timing seemed off. Of course, our carnal eyes will question timing, but there is never a conflict with Divine Order – never.

A new career in my Golden Years – why now? My computer acts up when I'm working on a deadline – why now? An unfavorable diagnosis from the doctor – why now? The health of my parent is failing – why now? A long lost friend surfaces – why now? To try to figure out God's timing is a waste of time. His thoughts and ways are not ours, and His timing definitely isn't ours. Again, there is never a conflict with Divine Order . It's all perfectly planned. We either believe it or we don't.

I have to remind myself that everything is not about me, so I shouldn't even entertain 'why now?' There are other people sharing the air I breathe and existing in this big world I live in. I have to get out of my selfish shell and stop asking what God's will is for *my* life, and simply seek His will – period. The circumstances surrounding me are also influencing the lives of those surrounding me. So, why now? Because God says so! Sounds just like something a parent would say, doesn't it? Our Heavenly Father knows best. Remembering this helps maintain peace through the storm. It won't be alright – It's *already* alright – right now!

One evening, feeling exhausted, I made a cup of hot tea with honey and ginger. I was thinking about the upcoming week and all I had to do, and it just made me more exhausted. As I submerged my tea bag in and out of the hot water, I remembered an email a friend forwarded to me. It referred to a woman being like a tea bag – you don't know her strength until she's in hot water. I felt like I had been submerged in hot water the entire week. After about ten long seconds, I quickly changed my mental channel. I didn't even want to *think* about what was coming up; I just wanted to enjoy that moment with my hot tea. I took another sip of my delicious green tea and said, "Lord, you got this, right?"

Although exhausted, strong emotions of gratitude flowed through me. I thought about my Strong Tower to lean on, my Shepherd to guide me, my Prince of Peace, my Comforter, my Keeper! All of a sudden my fatigue turned to unspeakable joy. Changing my mental channel was the key. It doesn't matter what's ahead because I don't have any control over it anyway. Women are strong – very strong, yet we easily become frustrated and fragile when we forget where our help comes from. When you feel like you've been submerged in hot water or in the midst of a turbulent storm, just ask "Lord, you got this, right?" Stay covered! Do whatever it takes for you to stay spiritually connected and maintain peace. Again, don't wait for the storm to hit – this can't be stressed enough!

"Therefore take up the whole armor of God, that you may be able to withstand in the evil day, and having done all, to stand."

Ephesians 6:13

When over land, the eye of a hurricane is the center of the storm. It is also the calmest part of the storm. When we maintain a spiritual eye in our storms, we too, will be calm. It's important to remain centered in our storms. When we're right in the middle of our storm and it appears all hell is breaking loose, God can deliver a calmness to our spirit. That calmness is actually His Spirit dwelling within us. Continual prayer keeps us centered, but outside influences distract us from our centered position. Remember those distractions Ms. Flesh travels with? Their main goal is to remove our focus. These distractions can keep us from what God has called us to do. Regardless of our age or what we're doing, focusing is key to success. As wives and mothers we must fight the Spirit of Distraction on a daily basis, so when a storm arrives we are already in a position to weather it.

Praise is what we do…even when we're going through. Praise is that precious part of our lives that gives us the power to get through storms regardless how severe they are. Yet for some reason, we don't ignite this power when in the midst of a storm. We've become so connected to the problem, we forget to praise. Praise isn't about calling on God and thanking Him for what He has done or can do, it's about acknowledging who He is.

I've been through some storms that didn't make any sense, yet I had that peace that surpassed all human understanding. This supernatural peace gave me a sense of confidence. I knew I was covered completely – from head to toe. I felt like I was in a spiritual bubble that couldn't be penetrated by the destructive hands of any man or weapon.

This peace may seem unattainable while in the midst of a storm, but that's the sole purpose of praise – to invite a connection with God. When we're in personal contact with Him, His words and promises are real to us, thus offering the strength our human nature lacks.

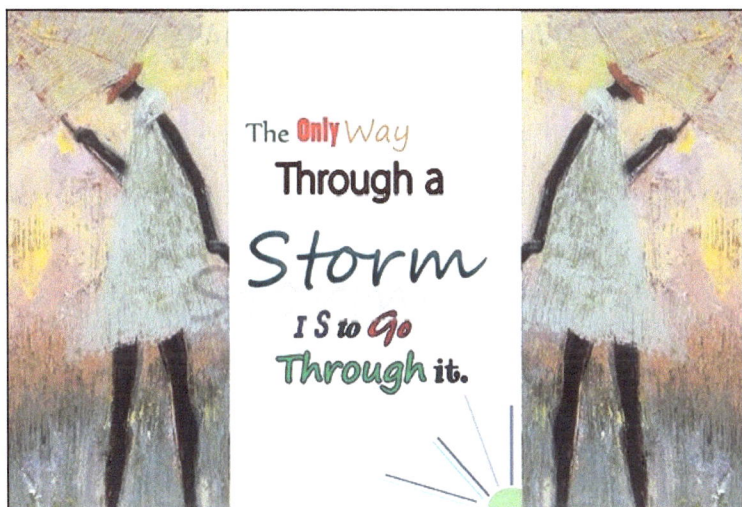

The **Only** Way
Through a
Storm
I S *to* 𝒢o
Through it.

Soul Storms

You may have never heard of a Soul Storm. It wasn't until I went through a few storms dealing with matters of the heart, like relationship matters, that I decided the painful, long lasting and severe storms were in a category of their own and deserved to be named; thus, Soul Storms. Soul Storms deliver turbulent winds like no other storm, and there is little or no time to prepare for them. These emotion-driven storms usually catch us in a comfortable state of mind with hearts unguarded.

There is a pill to relieve almost every ache and pain the human body experiences, but what about the aches and pains of the heart?. Wait a minute, can we actually *feel* a heart ache? What about love? Can we feel love in the heart? My scientific minded father reminds me that the heart is a muscular organ responsible only for pumping blood, through our veins, to the lungs and systems in the body. This is true, but the emotions we feel are real and are divinely connected to our physical heart and brain.

Whether we're dealing with grief, falling in or out of love, a pregnant teenage daughter, a son addicted to drugs, difficult co-workers, accomplishing a goal, or winning the lottery, emotions *will* be triggered. Soul Storms can develop from emotional wounds from decades past, or hurt feelings from yesterday. Memories from childhood abuse or insults, relationship rejections, mental abuse, marriage mess, and adversity invite discontent, unhappiness, anxiety, fear, panic, stress, disappointment, anger, hostility, sadness, depression, and other emotions with the potential to paralyze our will to endure.

Soul storms are exhausting. Every day can be a battle to endure. For some, it can be hard to get out of bed or live, for that matter. You may feel you're being held hostage by crippling thoughts that creep into the mind. It may take a continuous soul soak in scripture, affirmations, prayer and meditation to endure the treachery of a soul storm. If aggressive action isn't taken immediately after you recognize the storm, an unsafe connection to the issue may occur instead of a secure connection to the Creator. Once the connection is severed, the will to endure gradually vanishes without notice.

I remember a soul storm of my own, and wanting to encourage myself but couldn't find an ounce of courage to pour into my spirit. I knew I was covered, but I didn't feel connected. In the midst of the storm, I'd forgotten to rely on the strength of my Heavenly Father. I forgot about my little sister's text about "dem roots." Roots are important to a tree's survival, and my roots were crucial to my survival. It was during this Soul Storm that I understood others with addictions.

Addictions are compulsive and have the power to control us despite the consequences and a connection to a higher power is a must to overcome them. It calls for fasting and prayer, praise and worship, prayer and meditation, song and spiritual songs, affirmations and application of scripture, and whatever else you have stored in your storm prep kit. Yes, it takes all of that! Again, don't wait for the storm to prepare!

One thing about soul storms is that they reside so deep within the heart you'll want to wrap yourself up in a blanket of gloom and be perfectly content there. We blame it on the "enemy," but the enemy may be our own thoughts of despair, misery, pity, and pessimism – the enemy within. Soul storms reveal our weakness, but they also remind us of where our strength comes from!

When it comes to heartache from a broken relationship, all women have a storm to share. If not, "keep on livin." We've been lied to, cheated on, abused, misused, taken advantage of, or neglected, or maybe we've experienced a combination of them all. The bottom line is, our heart has been broken in one way or another as a result of a man's behavior. Whether we allowed the behavior or not, we've been hurt. Countless women have shared their heartaches with me, and I've experienced a few of my own, but I'll never forget this particular storm shared by a woman who found herself in a severe soul storm which lasted several years.

To protect her true identity, I refer to her as Tess. Tess is a beautiful, middle-aged, married woman with four children. She loved and supported her husband of ten years and created a happy home environment. Unfortunately, Tess noticed a few red flags in her marriage that set her intuition radar off. Unlike many women, Tess didn't ignore her intuition. She boldly addressed her "feeling," and although she had no proof, Tess confronted her husband. Admitting his adultery wasn't a problem, but unbeknownst to Tess, this wasn't his first time going astray. Tess chose to forgive her husband and their marriage was restored.

After a few months of renewed love, Tess found herself experiencing that "feeling" again. You know…that 'something ain't right' feeling. Instead of confronting her husband a second time, Tess entered a soul storm that almost physically killed her from the stress, worry, and constant mind battles she entertained. The stress invited health storms, which then invited financial storms. One thing led to another and finding the good in her storm was the furthest thing from her mind. Tess's husband eventually left the marriage, which left her distressed and depressed. Tess not only lost all hope for happiness, she lost her appetite, weight, and self worth. She struggled with getting out of bed each morning and eventually lost her job. The storm seemed to intensify, and the raging emotions not only shook her foundation, but her foundation cracked. Tess doubted God's love for her and questioned her connection with Him.

"Tired of being sick and tired," Tess was ready to fight the enemy of doubt and devastation in her own mind. After several months, Tess realized that fervent prayer was her only help. She was forced to lean and depend entirely on her Heavenly Father to get from one minute to the next. It was her spiritual covering that pulled Tess out of the dark pit she couldn't pull herself out of. She had become comfortable in the pit of despair and forgot the true source of her joy. Tess admitted she had not been in a storm for a long time. Things were "good." Little did she know her husband walking away allowed another man to walk into her life and appreciate in her, what her husband did not. Her financial storm slowly ceased after working two jobs for a while. Tess struggled for a while, but later found peace and happiness without the man she'd married – something she didn't think she'd be able to do.

I didn't share the details of Tess' storm, but I'm sure you get the idea. Please don't judge her. We all have a storm we're not proud of or maybe embarrassed to share. I'm sure many women can somehow relate to Tess' storm; I know I can. No matter how strong we appear on the outside, our heart is ripping apart on the inside, and the mask of happiness is securely placed. We smile through the pain and silently suffer.

If you're in a soul storm right now, please be assured it *will* pass. It can dissipate overnight, but some storms have the nerve to last longer. The one thing we can do is make up our minds to not marinate in the storm issue. Yes, it's difficult and it may feel like we're stuck, but we can get unstuck by being spiritually mindful and asking for supernatural help. We can't do it on our own. We have to change our mental channel and focus on Almighty God.

God knows exactly what category storm we need and how long it needs to last. He knows our strengths and weaknesses, and how to strategically place storms in our life to bring His plan to fruition.

"We know all things work together for good to those who love God..."

Romans 8:28

We either believe this or we don't. Look back for a minute, back on some of the situations in your life that didn't make sense. Hindsight will remind us that somehow, someway, the storm worked for our good. Even the sting of death teaches a powerful lesson. Through all the endless grieving and wavering emotions, death invites enlightenment.

Another type of soul storm I must mention is the death storm. A few courageous women have shared their storms with me and agreed to publicly share with you.

My Faith Went Where My Eyes Could Not See

Aundria Long Jackson, AL

Prior to June 22, 2004, I affectionately remember telling people I carry my faith and grace with me everywhere I go. I have spiritual faith and live under God's grace. But, the phrase had a double meaning for me because my daughters named Faith and Grace were literally with me most of the time. Whenever I mentioned my daughter's names or feasted my eyes upon them I was reminded of one of my favorite bible verses: Ephesians 2:8. "For by grace are ye saved through faith; and that not of yourselves: it is the gift of God." Faith and Grace were physical gifts from God, but, most importantly, God gave us all spiritual gifts of faith and grace.

My sweet seven year old daughter Faith went to heaven after a tragic car accident on June 22, 2004. I still don't understand why God allowed such a tragedy to happen. Words cannot express how much I miss Faith. BUT, I still stand FIRM in my declaration that I carry my Faith and Grace around with me. When my physical Faith went to heaven where my eyes could not see her; my spiritual faith went higher too, because this tragedy allowed me to witness first hand God's strength for the day, light for my way, and grace for my trials. I've witnessed his undying love in MY life.

If you've ever read the poem *Footprints in the Sand* then you can begin to understand how I felt hours and days after the accident. My earthly doctor recommended I take sedatives to alleviate the emotional pain, but, innately I knew I would become an addict if I could find a pill to remove the hurt that encompassed me. I made a conscious decision to rely on our heavenly doctor who has the antidote for every earthly woe.

The bible tells us in Psalm 55:22 to "Cast your cares on the LORD and he will sustain you; he will never let the righteous fall." I wept sporadically for days and called upon the name of our Lord and He sustained me. I rested in His arms and allowed Him to carry me through that most painful time of my life. No, I don't understand why God allowed this to happen, but, I remember meeting a mother at a park who had also lost a child, and she shared this with me: Life is like a piece of tapestry cloth. When you look at the bottom side of the cloth, it's just a bunch of strings that appear to lead nowhere. But, if you turn that same piece of fabric over a beautiful design is revealed. Our perspective can be equated to the bottom ugly side of the tapestry, but, God sees the top which is beautifully designed.

The more I study God's word, I catch a glimpse of the top tapestry. However, my earthly point of view can't begin to comprehend the artwork of an omnipotent God.

Grief is a difficult emotion. But, I wish I could push everyone to accept the plans the Lord has for us, and stomp on the devil. When we don't, we give the devil an underserved foothold in our lives. He came to kill, steal, and destroy. My wish for humanity is that we trust God when tragedy occurs. God's word tells us in Isaiah 40:31 "but those who hope in the Lord WILL renew their strength. They will soar on wings like eagles; they will run and not grow weary, they will walk and not be faint." I've found this verse to be true. When storms arise, place your hope in the Lord!

A Mother's Nightmare

Alicia Hobdy, FL

"Your wings were ready but my heart was not." It all started on January 5, 2013, when we went to check on our son Darius, our firstborn. He had visited with us on New Year's Day and said he thought he had the flu. He had not responded to our phone calls, so we went to his house to find him not feeling good, so we brought him home with us to take care of him. The next day was our wedding anniversary. We went to church leaving Darius to rest. Midway through the service, the mom in me got up to call the house to check on him. He didn't answer the phone, so we returned home to find him unresponsive.

Immediately I started praying as I am dialing 911. Paramedics are first to arrive and they, along with my husband, get him to respond for a minute. I hear one of the paramedics radio the hospital as to their estimated time of arrival. Having worked in the medical field, I knew this was not good. We arrived at the hospital and we were told his heart was not functioning properly, and that he had diabetic ketoacidosis, a life threatening condition. When they allowed us back to the room, we saw my son strapped to the bed. He'd become combative and non cooperative (sometimes an involuntary condition of a person in a diabetic emergency).

We learned from the EMT who transported him, that his glucose level was 1500. The highest they had ever experienced. He was admitted to ICU, and even as his mother, I wasn't allowed by his side 24/7, but only 30 minutes every 4 hours. He was admitted on Sunday but it was not until Wednesday that he was coherent enough to speak with us. But I saw all the signs that he wasn't improving but getting worse. He was not responding to medication, and his kidneys were shutting down. I asked God to help me understand his will. On Saturday the cardiologist explained they could not do the surgery on his heart because he was too weak and his vital organs were starting to shut down.

The staff started preparing us for his death. I called our other son Marc who was stationed in Germany preparing for his return to stateside duty, to let him know what was going on. As a mother, I was not there to give him that reassuring hug of love. Our youngest son Josef had come home from college to be with the family. Sunday morning, when we go back for our visit, the tears started to flow. The look my son gave me stays with me. He couldn't speak and was having trouble breathing. His eyes did the talking. I saw fear that he knew mom couldn't fix the situation.

The nurse came and said they were going to incubate him to help him breathe. Five minutes later, a Code Blue was called. My spirit told me it was Darius. Everyone was looking around the waiting room wondering whose family the code was called for. Ten minutes later the nurse came around the corner to get us. As we rounded the corner I could see the chaplain standing in the hallway with the nursing supervisor. Having worked at the hospital, I knew they were there for death notification. After they delivered the news, we prayed and went to be at Darius' bedside to say our goodbyes. I had the task of calling our son Marc in Germany to inform him of his brother's passing, and it was midnight there. He was very upset with his brother because like me, he felt that his brother knew about his heart problem and didn't tell family. I kept it together enough to give the American Red Cross information to get Marc home. I then had to contact Josef's friends to get him back to college as I was not letting him drive back by himself.

The three brothers had made plans once Marc had arrived back stateside in February.

Once I got home from the hospital, I totally lost it. I couldn't stop the crying as I recalled the memories. It is always said that the worst death to deal with is that of a child, and I can tell you, that this is the truth. The tears and smiles will come upon you at any time when you think of your child, and the emotions can really be worst around holidays and family events. As a mother, you never stop grieving or wondering if you told your child you loved them enough, and how proud you are of them. My son Darius was 32 when God called him home. I miss my bear hugs, his smiles, and him and his dad.

These words of another mother come to mind; that I must continue on, because I still have two sons who need their mother. I can't let grief take over my life. It was hard at one point dealing with the grief, and my own diagnosis of multiple sclerosis and losing my ability to walk, getting dressed, fatigue and pain. But now, I remind myself that Marc and Josef need their mother still.

Seeing the Sunshine Through the Storm

Barbara J. Stokes, FL

There are many storms of life that we go through, but I believe the biggest of those storms is the death of a loved one. In 2009, I lost a brother to gun violence, and in 2014, my husband lost his battle to stage 4 lung cancer. Those were some of the worst storms in my life. At one point in time, it was hard to recognize whether I was coming or going but whichever way I was going, I came to the realization that I could not stop moving, doing, praying and trusting in God. Because if I stopped during the onslaught of my life storm, I truly believed I would have been lost in a world of despair, depression and worthlessness.

During my husband's sickness, it was so hard watching him struggle each day to smile through his pain and push through his fear of dying. We discussed faith and the Will of God on many occasions, but I could still see the disbelief in his eyes relaying the "Why me Lord?" question. While sitting across from each other I saw tears in his eyes and I asked him; no I told him, that I knew he was afraid and it was okay to be afraid. But I also told him that as believers we should never lose hope even when death is staring us in our face.

This period in our lives felt like a tsunami- a strong tidal wave that shifts and destroys anything in its path; everything was shifting in our lives except our love and faith in each other and our trust in God. Losing someone that God had hand-picked just for you is no easy task.

If I had not been rooted in my faith, I believe that I would have lost my sanity, my will to fight or even pray. It was during the quite times soon after Charles' death, when I was totally alone, that my own words would echo back at me, reminding me of who/whose I am. *"Charles, God did not abandon you through your sickness; He's using you to strengthen someone else."* Those same words echo from my memory - God has not abandoned me through my storms - He is using me to help someone else see the sunshine through their storm. These thoughts help me get through days of loneliness and yes, sometimes a hint of despair.

"Storms May Rise, Winds Will Blow"

Tori W. W. McCollum, CA

Stealthfully, in the midnight hour of March 15th, He entered the bedroom, stepping over the plethora of pillows and blankets I had left on the floor, as if I could keep Him from entering our quiet, quaint domain. He rounded the slumbering berth, where my first heartbeat's barely, breathing body rested and whispered, "let's ride," and within an instantaneous moment (I noticed @ 12:15 a.m., but I believe it was long before then), my father stepped out of his earthly mortality and stepped into his empyrean immortality, and boarding his Chariot, he waved this side of Jordan "Goodbye, ride on King Jesus, no man cannot hinder me!" The Death Angel would enter the ranks of my family again, without my permission, precisely17 months and four days later and beckon for my second heartbeat; my beloved mother, who would squeeze my hand and at the same time, in genuflection, thank her Savior for eternal life and be reunited with her Soulmate on the morning of August 19th. My life hasn't been the same since.

My cell phone rang mid~mornin' on March 14, 2014 and by the lyrical tone, without even looking at it, I knew it was my endearing mother; checking on me, as we both did on a daily. However, in the last several days, we had been missing each other as she was caring for my father on a "round the clock" basis. I would travel to San Diego, CA; my childhood hometown; some sixty miles, one way from my northern residence, to assist her two or three times per week; whether I was leaving my managerial job or if I had the day off. My duties oftentimes consisted of preparing medicinal syringes for the next dosing administration, as Mommy's (yes at almost 47 years old, I still called her Mommy) hands sometimes shook from nervous anxiety.

"Good Mornin' Liebshin, what's your schedule like today?" "Mornin' Sweetie, tonight, I'm the Closing Manager, so I don't need to be at work until 4:00 p.m., is everything okay?" Her response, "do you think you could come spend a few hours with us before work? "Sure," was my reply, "I'll shower and get dressed for work and 'throw on my face,' and that way when it's time for me to go to work, I'll be ready to go." "Is everything okay?" I asked again. "It's not gonna happen today is it?" Tears had already begun to hasten into my larynx and my throat was beginning to seize, but as I waited for her answer, I knew she was preparing herself; steadying her vocal chords as she proceeded, "I'm not God, but I think you should come home." I knew my cherished, endeared, and esteemed father was sick; more sick then he wanted us to be cognizant of, as he had previously shared with me that his plethora of physicians had statistically predicted; six months. However, this was "Daddy," and if we continued our homeopathic care, which is something he was convinced would assist in his longevity, we could have more time. The day he shared his sixth month prognosis, I immediately started negotiating with God, "what are you doin' now, all these people doin' bad in this world, and now this, you want my father," but I continued to convince myself that we'd have six months (God gave us three), even longer if we just kept praying and seeking God's favor. I even beseeched the Lord as King Hezekiah did…and then Mommy's call and her quiet voice, "get here as soon as you can, but drive safely." "I'm on my way." I showered, quickly dressed, reached out to my "Road~Dawgs" who all resided where I was traveling to; Trudy, Henrietta, Belita, Natalie, and Millicent, by way of text and said, "I'm on my way home, things aren't looking good." Familiar with our health plight, each individually "hollered" back, "we're prayin', drive safely and keep us updated, we'll be there when you need us!"

I grabbed an overnight bag, but deep in the recesses of my heart, I felt, "everything's gonna be okay, I won't need this, I'll go for a few hours and be back in time to start my shift." I called my Management Team and shared "my latest," they'd been asking me on a daily basis about my father and each time, I'd say, "he's dying, but still strong" because really aren't we all dying just a little bit every day? Nevertheless, I struggled to believe my stronger than life, more powerful than Superman, so energetic, still agile, and virile father, just 71 years young was really dying. This was my coping mechanism, if things should take a turn for the worse and it seemed like it was doing just that. My Management Team instructed me, to get a move on and keep them informed, I promised I would and hit the door, runnin' like a scalded cat!! I recall choking back tears while the car idled, as I dialed my husband and asked if he could secure the boys' (we have three) transportation from school, and off I went into the morning sun and calm breeze, careful not to be so trepid that I broke speed barriers, incurring a traffic violation. Nothing feels worse than traveling and wondering minute by minute what's going on with a loved one's failing health.

I arrived at the front door of our home and noticed a note in my mother's hand~writing, "come on in." "Yikes," I thought and a few other explicatives, "this must be really bad if she's left the front door unlocked and can't afford the time to answer it," I entered the eerily entry way and quietly announced my arrival to which her sweet response encouraged me to come where she was. The sun reflected brightly off the iridescent, panoramic ocean view, as I took in the sight of my tall, handsome father, bed~ridden and whispering while trying to smile, "Hello, Daughter, your mother is busy, fussin' over me. You should take her for some lunch, bring me some Dumpling Soup, I'll be fine." A dear family~friend; Harold Tolson was also there, massaging swollen feet and ankles to increase blood flow. All three of us would chime in together, "nobody's going anywhere." It was at that moment, my job wasn't the priority, my father was dying right before my very eyes. I wept uncontrollably in my mother' arms, in a separate room so as not to alert my father of the sheer melancholy I was feeling, nor did I want him to worry. Even in the midst of his dying, he was concerned about us.

And so it would be, seventeen months later, when Mommy and I received the news that we would not be healed on this alluvial side, it would be me again weeping without consolation. "God, really, you know I'm the only child and here you go again, have I not met my quota?" Mommy would scoop me up in her arms and tell me, "you can do this, be strong my Daughter." Id' move home within the ensuing months and Hospice Care would come with their schedule of arrival times. Bathing and oral hygiene would be done bedside, prescriptions for comfort would be administered by me and now it would be me scooping Mommy in my arms, caring for her, talking to her at every juncture, telling her how much I loved her, she in turn crying because she couldn't respond.

When she lost her ability to swallow, I would massage the side of her throat as if taking her pulse and when that stopped working, syringes to assist prescriptions down her cheek line would come into fruition. Medicine would be crushed between spoons and mixed with apple juice to allow an easier trickling down the throat passage. I resembled a veteran drug addict. Daily, I watched, praying she wasn't suffering, the quiet drone of the oxygen machine keeping "tabs" on breathing. Mommy's outward appearance would change each day and as I moisturized her "shedding" body, I knew then that Almighty God was preparing her new one. She exhaled while I was talking to her, "go get your two MEN," culminating her old life, her new life; everlasting commencing.

The title of this tome, beautifully written by my endearing friend; LaVender was created I believe for such a time as this. "When Hell Breaks Loose - How To Weather The Storms Of Life" is apropos for any individual who is struggling through a storm or preparing for one. If you've never been there; praise God, but keep on living…it's on the way. In the meantime, those who are in the midst of an unrelenting storm, you may need to seek counsel; grieving classes, spiritual guidance, but stand strong despite the waves that are crashing and flooding your quintessential soul. Rest assured that our Captain has it ALL in His control…our ships were built for this, let Him steer you into safe harbor. See you there!

"A strong woman knows she has strength for the journey, but a woman of strength knows that it is in the journey that she will become strong."

Author unknown

Post Storm

Have you ever stopped to notice the beauty in the sky after a rainstorm has just ended? The sky is clearer, and the crisp aroma to me, is like clean earth(whatever that smells like) that should be bottled and sold as laundry detergent. I'm not an expert, but I was curious enough years ago to research this unusual "after the storm" beauty. The beauty in the sky and the fresh earthy aroma known as petrichor, are a combination of the ozone, plant oil that has been secreted, and a chemical compound from bacteria in the soil. A process of these factors working together causes the beauty after a storm.

The spiritual storms we encounter are not much different. After a storm, spiritual eyes see clearer and the mind is renewed with a fresh dose of God's wisdom and knowledge. We are awakened and anew. There may be some scars, but those battle wounds remind us that God's grace was and is sufficient. We wanted to be rescued from the storm, but instead we reluctantly endured it. And guess what? We're still here! After a few storms, we have a better understanding of the benefits of staying covered.

Because storms deliver increased knowledge and courage, each one should better prepare us for the next. Hindsight is a good tool for preparation. Take a minute and look back at your past storms. Can you think of any storm that God has not brought you through? Did you come out of the storm stronger and wiser?

I remind you of what I went through on my job. After that severe storm passed, I can look back and see that although it was one of the most difficult times of my life, it was unbelievably rewarding. Many life lessons were learned and I received countless blessings, and the blessings continue to come.

I tried my best to escape the storm, and even considered quitting my job. I remember whining and crying about it to a couple of people, but was persuaded to stick with it by "wise counsel." I reluctantly continued showing up for the most difficult job I've ever had. There were just way too many moving parts and details for me. I knew my boss, Mr. Hill, needed someone sharper or maybe even younger than I, yet he obviously saw something in me that I didn't. When I made mistakes, he forgave them. When I forgot tasks, he reminded me. To this day, I thank Mr. Hill for his patience with me. I got so sick of being corrected, I was convinced he either desperately needed help or recognized my potential. There were days he was frustrated with me – I know, but he remained patient. I prayed and cried, prayed and cried. Mr. Hill probably did, too. To this day, I continue to thank Mr. Hill for my job that I wanted to quit. Not only am I learning a new career, but Mr. Hill has set me up for a future in other areas in radio – a career I never even thought of.

It's safe to say that the mental hell I took myself through, were my own doubts and fears of my ability to fill my present position. I didn't blame it on the "enemy." The enemy was within – within me. Too often, we talk ourselves out of the very things meant for us. I almost talked myself out of my future! I wanted to be delivered from the storm that was strategically designed to work in my favor. The storm put me in a position to securely stand on my own two feet after walking away from a 20 year marriage. I walked right into my destiny. Not only did Mr. Hill bless me, but my two sons benefit, too. I could go on and on about Mr. Hill and the direct and indirect ways my life has been touched by *his* radio station. Yes, Media One Communications (CHOICE 106.9 FM & 980 WRNE AM) is owned and operated by Mr. Robert Hill.

The knowledge I've gained through my storm has allowed not only a new career, but a new life! We desire to be stronger and more courageous, yet we fight going through the process to be stretched. Grapes have to be squeezed or pressed to get the juice. I was definitely squeezed and pressed. I was also rearranged and changed – for the better. I'm still prayerful while at work. I can't afford to get comfortable because I'm still learning and I still make mistakes and forget, but thank God not as often. I'm positive Mr. Hill is thanking God, too!

When the rain stops, the increase continues.

Hindsight *is* a blessing, but it can also hinder our spiritual outlook. How, you ask? When we look back on past storms, we see only what God has brought us through. We fail to see God as an ALMIGHTY God. Our thoughts are limited to only what we've seen with our carnal eyes. We limit God by remembering only what we've allowed Him to do through our finite thoughts instead of remembering his ALMIGHTY power which supersedes our human imagination. I need to say it again. God is ALMIGHTY. He changed water to wine. He made the blind man see. He healed the woman with the issue of blood. He brought Lazarus back to life. He gave laVender a new career in her golden years. So, why do we doubt God performing miraculous acts in our life? God not only supplies our needs, but He can supply in abundance if we don't limit Him. He came to give us life in abundance. I don't know any parent who is rich that has their child living in poverty. Our Heavenly Father is a King and we are His daughters.

The umbrella paintings within this book and on the cover are more than just my sister's art that I admire. Each umbrella reminds me of my covering. No matter what the issue of the storm is, these colorful umbrellas remind me of my protection. I have a large umbrella painting in my living room titled Divas Reign, and when I walk in and out the front door, it reminds me that I'm covered by the love of God. There is nothing that God hasn't brought me through – nothing, so why worry about any storm that's predicted for my life. I'm covered and I'll make it through. It won't be alright…it's already alright!

The following devotionals are taken from my files of Monday Meditations, which I share through email each Monday morning. Some are from my early days of mothering two young sons and others are more recent.

Basically, I'm sharing my storms with you. Storms strengthen – especially when we share our umbrella.

My Struggle

One of the most severe storms I've been through was a financial storm. When I chose to disconnect from my 20 year marriage, I knew it would be hard. Although retired military and newly employed at my current job, I struggled! I'm convinced that limited or no finances is one of the reasons many women stay in marriages they aren't happy in. I didn't say *the* reason, I said, *one of the* reasons. Well, my happiness was more important than a dollar, so I accepted the invitation to struggle. I was a homemaker for eleven years before getting a job outside the home. I wasn't responsible for paying utility bills and groceries. I had to purchase a car which meant car maintenance. My two teenage sons were with me, so I had their needs to provide for as well. They watched their mama struggle, but you know what? They watched God work in my life also. I went from eating fish sticks everyday to being able to take my boys out to eat. I went from driving only where I needed to go to keeping a full tank of gas in my car. I went from writing books to owning a publishing company. I went from lying to my parents that everything was alright to actually being alright. That's not all! The Lord blessed me with male friends that are always there for me. I call them my angels in suits although sometimes they are over protective and borderline father-like. I've never had to ask them for anything, but knowing I have loving safety nets around me reminds me of the inconceivable love God has for me. I struggle no more. Was it difficult? It was hard as hell, but worth watching God be God and keep His promises. The Lord is my shepherd, I shall not want – for NO THING.

Are You Ready?

I looked out the window one morning expecting to see windy, rainy conditions since public school was canceled. My city was under a hurricane warning, but the weather had been so beautiful, it was hard to imagine imminent storm conditions. That morning, a lot of people were watching and praying in regards to the hurricane and trailing tornadoes. Regardless of where the hurricane hits, most people will prepare – just in case. The direction of hurricanes is so unpredictable, so preparation is key. I thought about being under storm watch as it relates to my own spiritual life. I never know what area of my life a storm may hit, but one thing is guaranteed – it w*ill* hit. The direction and intensity of my storms always change and there is always that calm before each one, which has the tendency to trick me and allow the storm to catch me off guard. I know from past storms, that I needed to prepare and have my ear and eye gates guarded and secure. Every aspect of my life needed to be covered with prayer and I needed my battle gear on and secure. I know to watch and pray. Hurricane and tornado watches are necessary, and so are spiritual storm watches. You may not live in the path of a tropical storm, but your life is in a direct path to get hit. Are you ready? If not, it's time to prepare! I now place you under storm watch; get ready!

Sounds of Nature

I woke up to the sound of rumbling thunder, pounding rain, and lightening flashing through the windows. It's been a long time since I've heard all three of these powerful elements at the same time. While listening to the sounds of nature, I thought about the children who are afraid of these sounds and run to their parents' bedroom for comfort and protection. I also wondered what explanation the parents give when the children ask where these sounds come from. Do we tell them how the temperature and the humidity have to be in sync? Do they tell them about the negative charge in the clouds? Do we tell them particular clouds must form before a thunderstorm occurs, or do we say, "God made it." Both answers are correct, yet what a great opportunity to recognize the awesomeness of God in the scientific dynamics of nature. Watch the sky when it lights up from lightening; that's electricity! Watch the sun when it sets. Watch the drops of rain as they fall – only God! Have you ever thought about the process rain drops go through to produce snow or how a rainbow is created? It doesn't just happen, and man isn't smart enough to create such an amazing act of nature. Let's not forget the wind. Who can create something we can feel, but can't see? Only the amazing creator of the heavens and the universe is capable of such beautiful art. I stand in awe as I look at the art of nature around me and listen to the sounds it makes. Stop for a minute and look out your window. What do you see? A canvas of beautiful art created by the same God that created you! We shall behold Him!

Stop, Drop, and Pray

"You must have a lot of patience." This is what mothers would say when they found out I homeschooled my two sons for several years. Uh, patience has never been one of my strong traits. During the course of a normal day of homeschooling, anything can happen. On top of keeping the boys on track and focused, the phone rings, cleaning and cooking needs to be done, attitudes need to be suppressed, and sibling rivalries require controlling. When things get out of hand, I would yell, "Stop, drop, and pray!" The boys knew to stop whatever they were doing, drop to their knees and we would pray. We weren't praying about anything in particular, just simply acknowledging God in our day. It didn't matter how many times a day, if I was led to stop, drop, and pray, I did. As mothers, it's so important to teach our children the importance of communicating with God and even more important to acknowledge and *listen* to God. How easy is it to go half the day and realize we've only had morning prayer? I don't know about you, but I need God every minute of the day. Teaching children how to establish a connection with their Creator is one of the best gifts we can give them, and age doesn't matter. There are adults still learning how to connect with God, so if children create this habit of prayer early in life, they'll know to stop, drop, and pray when life gets out of hand. How's *your* day going? Is God calling you to stop, drop, and pray? Now is a good time.

Stinky Advice

Why are you doing this? Maybe you should do that. Don't fight that battle. These are just a few comments I've received while going through the storms of life, but taking heed to what others say isn't important to me. Hearing God's voice and trusting Him is. Nothing God leads me to do makes sense to me, so I don't expect anyone else to understand my actions. When I begin to listen to others, I compromise and doubt God's voice. Yes, God can speak through others, yet I still must recognize His voice for myself. Call me crazy, strange, or even a radical, but I know my God's voice, and it has never led me wrong - never. My father told me advice is like old fish and sour milk; it stinks and nobody wants it. It's so easy to give someone else advice about their life, but when we look at our own life, it's close to being messed up from the floor up.

The best advice is to direct the person to *the* Advisor. Hearing God's voice and *trusting* His voice assures confident choices regardless of what other voices are saying. It's not easy following a voice that doesn't make sense, but each time I trust Him, I'm glad I did and it helps trusting Him the next time easier. The doubts slowly fade away. God's ways and thoughts are not ours, which is a clear indication our choices are wrong if we aren't led by His Spirit. We're instructed not to lean to our own understanding, but to acknowledge Him in all our ways. Now *that's* good advice!

My Situation

I had a conversation with someone about 'the situation' Joseph was in when he found out his virgin fiancé, Mary, was pregnant. We brought 'the situation' to the present and discussed what Joseph's home boys would have told him, and what we would've thought if Joseph was a friend of ours. Would we tell Joseph to trust God or would we be in his ear stirring up mess and confusion? We all have a situation we're dealing with. I have a few situations of my own. It seems like the more intimate I become with God, the more situations arise. *Good grief!* One thing that helps me through my situations is remembering my life is not my own. I was created with specific purpose, so when 'situations' arise, they can direct me to the path God chose for me. I believe I was created *by* Him *for* Him with a *perfect* plan for my life. My 'situations' have a way of getting my attention and keeping me in prayer. My situations remind me of the Holy Spirit waiting to give guidance and direction. My situations remind me to trust God and not lean to my own twisted understanding. Situations are good things if we look at them through spiritual eyes. If not, our carnal eyes make our 'situation' devastating and mentally exhausting as we try to come up with a solution. I choose to be like Joseph and not listen to people in my ear, but trust God. God promised to take care of me, right? He told me to follow Him, right? He said ALL things work together, right? Situations can either draw us closer to the Creator or drive us away from Him. Where is your 'situation' taking you?

Are You Praying?

I usually awake with fragments from a lingering dream on my mind, or with thoughts of yesterday, but this morning when I awoke, my mind was already in prayer mode. I've never experienced this before, so I took this spiritual awakening to mean I needed an extra layer of prayer, so the Spirit started praying for me before I awoke. We all need an extra layer of prayer, which is why we're instructed to pray without ceasing. We all have an issue or a problem we're working through and often wonder if we're making the right decisions. My life is full of challenges right now, and I can't imagine living without prayer. With each changing season of my life, a new season and level of prayer is invited. As I mature in age, the woman in me just wants to make self happy. Beginning a new career in my golden years has invited constant prayer. Having a son in the Army stepped up my prayer life. My aging parents call for more prayer. I've had a prayer partner for years, but all of us should make prayer our partner, our BFF, our ride or die buddy, our side kick, our go to partner, our right hand. In my younger years, prayer was just a word – something I did, but now prayer is my avenue to making sound decisions. Prayer is my lifeline, my connection to my Power Source. Prayer is my peace of mind! Whatever situation we're facing or whatever storm we find ourselves in, prayer is our pathway to guidance, but let's not forget prayer is a two-way conversation. After we pray, we must listen. Stormie OMartian says it best in her books, "Shut up and pray!"

Wake It Up

One morning while meditating, I was reminded that the Spirit of the living, majestic GOD lives inside me. Imagine this for a minute. The same God that created the heavens and the universe left us with His Spirit and it resides in us. It's almost scary when you *really* think about it. We have the power of a *living* God inside us. There is no need for us to ever be in a position that we are overwhelmed with the cares of this world or living without direction and peace of mind. The Spirit of an omnipotent God rests and resides within us. Maybe that's the problem – it's resting. Are we using the Spirit of God enough or maybe we don't know how to use it. Is it sitting dormant and waiting to be stirred up while we whine, cry, and pray for God's help? He gave us His Spirit – can He give us anything more? I know I probably use just a fraction of His power in me, but when I awoke this morning, I realized something. I had been sleeping for almost eight hours, so of course my organs and brain needed time to realize they weren't working in sleep mode anymore. I even drank some water to help my brain cells and organs get in gear. I slowly felt my mind and energy being renewed. The same is with the Spirit of God living in us. We have to activate it or it will simply rest – all day. The power is waiting for us to stir it up with prayer and praise. If not, it will be in rest mode and we will be spiritually weary all day. We have power! Supernatural power! Wake it up! Stir it up! Live in the Spirit of God

The Best Part

There's a jingle for coffee stuck in my mind. I believe it's a Folgers commercial and it says, "The best part of waking up is Folgers in your cup!" I'm not a coffee drinker, I'm a tea girl, but the catchy, coffee jingle took me somewhere I'd like to stay. It's the first part of the jingle that spoke to me. The best part of waking up…hmmm…in my mind, the best part of waking up is realizing I'm awake. I don't need to go through the rest of the day to find out what kind of day I'll have because the best part is waking up. Can the day get any better? When I think about the alternative to waking up, it makes me want to shout! I'm here another day in spite of my mess on yesterday. Thank you, Lord! It's a new day that I haven't seen before and as it unwraps itself, I dare not complain about the light afflictions that will try to steal my focus. I dare not allow OPP, other people's problems, to create drag in my day. I dare not waste time thinking about yesterday's issues and miss out on the blessings of today. I dare not allow trash thoughts to suffocate my peaceful thoughts of the gift of life. Oh yes, the best part of my day is definitely waking up. No doubt, there are guaranteed traps and snares set to try to ruin my day, so how do I plan to maintain this joyful mindset? There is only one way…by staying connected to my Creator. The second half of the jingle just came to me, but I have my own words. The best part of waking up, is Jesus in my life. Now *that's* a jingle!

Recall

Have you ever had a day when everything went wrong? Well, several things happened one weekend that had the capability of making me lose it. I'll spare you the details of my stormy weekend because I'm sure you have a storm or two of your own to deal with. How do I know? Well, it's called life and there is no escaping it; however, we can escape the dark emotions and mindset that often accompanies storms of life. With each incident that happened, I was reminded who was in control, that I could do all things through Christ, and that greater is He who is in me than he who is in the world. I was reminded where my help comes from, to count it all joy, to trust and believe, to dwell in the secret place, to abide, to praise while I'm going through. With every thought of defeat, a promise of hope counteracted and restored my peace. It was a constant battle this weekend, but God! At the end of my Monday Meditations are two words - perfect peace. God promised if I keep my mind on Him, He would *keep* me in perfect peace. My peace is my stable ground through my chemically imbalanced thoughts and ways. My peace is my reminder that everything is *already* alright. My peace may be shaken, but it will never be shattered as long as I reflect on God's promises. When going through, if we just life our hands and praise God, we walk covered and connected in His love and protection – regardless of what life delivers. No need to recall the day, just call on Him.

Retreat

No, I'm not having a retreat, but I'm sure the word captured your attention. Women desire and maybe even need periodic getaways because so much falls on our shoulders – everybody needs us. I returned from a much needed weekend getaway and was welcomed home with a slap back into reality. I had to quickly go on another retreat, a mental retreat, to shake the weird mood I felt coming over me. It wasn't a bad mood, but a mood that wanted to still be out of town with no responsibilities and no hats to wear. Selfish? Maybe, but isn't the purpose of a retreat to help us practice being a little selfish. Getting away renews the mind and body, and restores the energy and strength needed to endure the realities of life. I don't know about you, but it's not in my budget to get away as much as I desire, which is why I take mental retreats. I sometimes imagine myself in the mountains or near a large body of water where I can hear only the waves. I never stay long on these mental retreats because it doesn't take long to shake the need for escape. I used to feel guilty for wanting to escape, but when I consider the complexities of being a woman, the guilt disappears. Is it time for you to get away? Go! Can't afford it? Take a quick mental retreat and escape to renew your mind. Your family will thank you.

Pass the Test

Years ago, I had Secondborn take several practice driving tests to prepare him for his learner's permit test. He passed some and he failed some. I assured him if he took enough practice tests and studied enough, he'd pass; and if he didn't, he could always take the permit test again. Yes, it costs to take and retake the actual test, but it's okay – children cost. I thought about the life tests that I've faced on my spiritual journey. Some tests I pass and some I fail. The ones I fail continue to re-surface again and again and the circumstances behind the tests pop up in my mind more than I care to think about them. Thank goodness it doesn't cost any money to retake these life tests, but it does cost time and energy. I always get tested in my weak areas. My main issue is being selfish with my time, plus I love my own company; so you can imagine some of the tests I fail. Selfishness has been my issue all my life. I asked my father when he first noticed my selfishness. He remembered me picking up my toys and going in the house when other children came to play with me. *WHAT?!* So, was I born selfish or did I learn selfishness? Regardless of when it started, I know better and *should* do better. We all have an idea of what our weaknesses are and should prepare for the tests. How do we prepare? By staying close to God and learning His character instead of displaying our own. We prepare by staying connected to Him and abiding in Him. I get tired of dealing with some things over and over again, and I definitely get tired of the same tests, but this is my fault. With each test, I have a choice - pass or fail. There's a test coming for you today, also…hope you pass!

Head in the Clouds

While taking a walk one day and enjoying the fresh air, I noticed the sky was full of beautiful, white clouds. I looked directly over my head and the only dark cloud in the sky was right above me. *What the....?!* Of course I attempted to walk away from it, but it was either following me or it was just one huge cloud. It was sorta funny, but the twisted part of my brain wondered if I had a dark cloud hanging over my head and never noticed it. A few seconds later, all the clouds begin to move, including the dark cloud; and guess what I saw? A rainbow!

The rainbow was small and the colors were very pale, but it brought me so much joy. Isn't if funny how rainbows make us smile? Even children get excited when they see a rainbow. I kept watching the clouds move around and realized how similar the puffy clouds are to the issues in my life. Some are big, some are small, and some are darker than others, but one thing my issues and clouds have in common is that they *always* pass. As the clouds continued to shift in the sky, they eventually covered my already faint rainbow. Again, I compared what was happening in the sky to my life. I can choose to focus on the dark cloud or the colorful rainbow that is hidden behind it. Whether I see the rainbow or not... behind every dark cloud is a silver lining. What does this mean to me? No matter what clouds (issues) come my way, they will pass. I may have had my head in the clouds during this walk, but the life lesson I received took me to new heights! This too, shall pass!

Don't Stop

I usually exercise on my own, but one evening I decided to step out of my comfort zone and attend a group exercise session led by a physical fitness trainer. When I saw the trainer, I knew I was in trouble, so I stood in the back to prevent embarrassing myself. The session started with jumping jacks, which I do every day – piece of cake! I completed the jumping jacks and was ready to move on to the next exercise. I was pumped. As the young folks say, I was turned up! The exercises continued and gradually became more difficult - so much for my piece of cake. In the middle of the session, I was secretly calling the personal trainer crazy. *What the heck is he thinking?* I despise floor exercises and they almost killed me. Sometimes I stopped in the middle of the sets, rested, and picked up with the last few. I was exhausted and wanted to leave, but I stayed. Some exercises were harder than others, so I just did what I could. While trying to lift my leg in some awkward position, I began to think of the many things I've gotten tired of and quit. Whatever the case may be – relationships, career, children, writing a book, saving money, and even my exercise regime…the only way I can lose is if I stop. We all have something we've considered throwing the towel in on. I've thrown many a towel in. Since that exercise class, I've joined a gym, but no personal trainer. I know what my goal is, so I will not stop. On days I don't feel like going, I think about that grueling group exercise. I wanted to quit, but I didn't. Whatever it is we're enduring, we can do this! Don't stop!

Oh My God!

Firstborn has never been a party-goer, but last nig ɩ he and a couple of his basketball teammates went to a party thrown by another teammate. Firstborn and I prayed before he was picked up; we didn't allow him to drive. I also reminded him about his "no" to drugs and alcohol. He left, and I was at peace. I was the designated after-party, pick up parent and was led to leave the house an hour early. I found a great parking spot right on the corner in eye's view of the building. Not even two minutes later, I heard what I thought to be gunshots, and people were running away from the party and in the streets, but shortly they began to return. Okay, maybe those weren't real gunshots. I then heard more gunshots – I know what I heard. Before I knew it, the entire block was covered with young people running with fear on their faces, cars screeching off, cell phones lighting up, and soon the police showed up with lights flashing. All I could think about was my child and before I knew it, I yelled, "What the f…!" I looked around in disbelief that I was in the middle of gunfire. I sat in my car paralyzed with confusion. *Is this happening?* With my heart beating fast, I selfishly prayed that my son and his teammates would find the car in the midst of the confusion and uncontrolled crowd. It seemed like forever, but the three of them were *finally* walking towards the car – thank you, Jesus! When they got in the car, I exhaled with great relief, and got the heck out of the area. It was silent for a few seconds and then we all began to talk. Never in my life have I experienced anything like that. I asked if anyone prayed and one young man said he did. Firstborn said, "All I could say was, oh my God." Firstborn's first response was much better than mine! Mothers, if you don't already cover your children in prayer, please start; and more importantly, teach them to cover themselves in prayer. We don't always know where our children are or who they are surrounded by, but God's merciful hands of protection will always surround them – it's their covering! Last night, Firstborn met the Protector up close and personal; things could have been a lot worse. Life lesson? Pray, mothers…pray.

Slow Down

Firstborn and I were standing in a self-checkout lane a while ago although our line was shorter than others, it was moving extremely slow. The machines kept locking up, which meant customers were becoming agitated. I thought I was going to rush in and rush out, but that didn't happen. The lady behind us was growing extremely impatient and was verbally trying to process the long wait. She was trying her best to stay calm, and we heard her say softly, "You gotta have patience." As soon as we got to the register, Firstborn said, "Slow down." He didn't want us to lock the machine up and be held up. I thanked him for his adult-like instruction, and we proceeded with our two items. Almost immediately, we heard an extremely loud bang that startled everyone in the store. We looked around and noticed the woman behind us had walked into an emergency exit door, shattered it, and fell out!

We don't know how badly she was hurt, but she wasn't moving. We both stood in shock as store employees rushed to her assistance and called for help. We finished our checkout, without the machine locking up, and passed by the lady on the floor, surrounded by employees. The lady was in a hurry to go somewhere, but went nowhere. Life is the same way. No matter how much we rush, everything happens in its own time and we have no control. We grow anxious for certain days to come and can't wait for other days to pass by. We watch the clock, can't wait for red lights to change, and look forward to uncomfortable seasons in our life to pass by – not knowing what's ahead of us. We're only rushing our life away. Aren't the days passing by quickly enough on their own? The lady behind us was obviously rushing; but her next few minutes in life weren't worth the rush. For the love of life, slow down. What's the hurry?

Moment By Moment

Here it is again….another Monday! One good thing about this Monday is the new opportunity I have to react to unforeseen circumstances with an optimistic attitude. Just as sure as I am breathing, there are several traps set to attempt to ruin the day. Running late, a slow child, traffic, complainers, long red lights, an unexpected meeting, an email, or even a phone call may alter my mood. I don't even know which thoughts will pop into my mind to attempt to take me to a dark place I'd rather not go. One thing I know for sure is that the outcome of today is up to me. I can choose to get caught up in the moment with an ugly attitude or I can choose to allow the supernatural power of God to consume me - moment by moment. Every step I make and every breath I take is a reminder that I am not my own. I am alive this Monday to allow the majestic power of God to dwell within me and touch the lives of those around me. I am alive to have an attitude of gratitude. I am alive to find the good and the God in all my circumstances. I am alive to have a heart and mind of thanksgiving for all God has done and will do in my life. I am alive to live! To live an abundant life of joy, peace, and happiness regardless of my circumstances! How am I supposed to keep this optimistic outlook? Moment by moment. Say it with me – moment by moment – moment by moment – moment by moment. Allowing God to have His way with us and through us, moment by moment, is the act of abiding, and He promised to abide in us if we abide in Him – moment by moment.

Counting Pennies

Years ago, I remember driving to worship service and asking the boys if they had any money, and they didn't. I didn't have a penny. I hate it when the offering plate goes around and no one has anything to offer. There is always some change in my purse, so I started digging for coins. I came up with several pennies, a safety pin, a mint, and some lint. I dug a little deeper and came up with a few silver coins and more pennies. I showed Firstborn my handful of coins and he shook his head and smiled. His head shake made me wonder if I should give my pennies or just throw them back in my purse. I could have written a check, but it would have immediately bounced in the usher's face. I chuckled at the pressure I was putting on myself to give, then recalled the Bible story of the poor widow who gave all she had, two mites. I'm not a widow, nor was I poor, but at that particular time, I sure had more month than money and the change I found was all I had. I whispered to Firstborn, "God doesn't look at the amount, He looks at the heart." Although I said that to Firstborn, I was really encouraging myself and making it okay to give my pennies. I may have more month than money, but God has always been my sufficiency – *always,* and He comes through in ways I never expect. We had a refrigerator and cabinets full of food, a full gas tank, money in the boys' lunch accounts, shelter, and clothes. The only thing I needed was trust in God. As long as I keep my eyes on Him, I have *everything* I need. I may have had only pennies to count, but when I count my blessings, they are plentiful!

Fill Me Up

At 4:30 one morning, I sat and thought to myself, "I don't feel like cooking a pot of grits or flipping pancakes this morning." It was early, but that was the time God always has and still wakes me to spend time with Him. My Bible and devotional books were next to me waiting to be cracked open, so I did. I sat and read about Paul and his amazing commitment to Christ. Paul's entire life was completely consumed by Jesus, and there I was complaining about cooking grits. I bet Paul didn't have to get up in the morning and cook breakfast. I'm sure he had the liberty to wake up and fall on his face in prayer for as long as he wanted to. Excuses, excuses, excuses. I could have gotten up to fall on my face also, if I want to. My life can also be committed to Christ. What does cooking breakfast have to do with it? Absolutely nothing. A complaining spirit wanted to control my thoughts. It started early, didn't it? One complaint about cooking breakfast would have led to another complaint, and another, and another. If I don't awake early to spend time with God and allow His Spirit to fill me up, I'm full of junk - complete negativity – trash thoughts! Yuck! I can hardly stand myself when I'm like that, so how would anyone else stand me? My prayer every morning is for God to hide me from myself and cover me with His Spirit of love, joy, compassion, mercy, understanding, longsuffering, and any other characteristic of Christ, but not my own! After I finished reading and praying, I felt like cooking breakfast. My mind was renewed. A little consecrated, contemplated time with God goes a long way. Trust me; I know! My mind is on Him now, not myself. Now, excuse me while I cook breakfast for my family.

Let It Go

The longer I live, the more I realize who God is. Just when I thought I knew the power of God, I found out I didn't know jack crap! Every day brings new issues. Every season brings new storms. Every stage of my life and the life of my children invites new levels of growth. I've been weathering a line of storms which are trying to shake my foundation, but because of past storms, I know not to lean to my own understanding, but to just let it go. It took me years to understand what 'letting go' meant. It doesn't mean my storm will dry up and go away, but my peace in the storm will allow me to stand strong and keep my head up, which I like to call poise – this is letting go. It doesn't mean the storm won't be painful, but my faith in the storm will remind me of my Comforter – He wants me to let it go. It doesn't mean I'm supposed to just sit and do nothing, but I'm to pray without ceasing and continually praise God through my storm – praise helps to let it go. My storm shouldn't be magnified, but my storm should invite God to be magnified - this is letting go. I'm so thankful my foundation is anchored in God because as the fierce winds try to cause damage in my faith, my trust in God makes riding the storm easier. When I let go and let God have His way, peace finds its way to me – perfect peace. There is a storm moving your way…prepare to let it go!

Boring Bible

The title sounds like blaspheme doesn't it? Well, I use to think the Bible was boring. Every time I picked it up, the thous and shalts bored me to tears and I never knew where to begin reading. I would find every excuse not to read the Bible. *Booooring!* As I grew older and wiser, I realized how much I needed God's presence in my life. I dare not start my day without His Word. If you ever want to start reading the Bible and not know where to start, The Psalms are awesome! The Psalms, located right in the center of the Bible, remind me that God is the center of my life and He keeps me centered in the midst of my storms. The center of the storm is where the storm is most calm.

Reading the Psalms has given me a deeper relationship with God. This morning, I read Psalm 27 and it began with, "The Lord is my light and my salvation, whom shall I fear? The Lord is the strength of my life, of whom shall I be afraid?" I read a little further, and it read, "Hear, O Lord, when I cry with my voice: have mercy also upon me, and answer me." I continued reading with, "Wait on the Lord; be of good courage; and he shall strengthen thine heart; wait, I say on the Lord." Now, what woman doesn't need these words in her life today? Boring Bible? I don't think so! How we react to daily situations reveals how much Word we have in our life - our Word level. As we deal with our toddlers, teenagers, and adult children, God's Word gives us power! As wives help their husbands, God's Word gives them power! As we interact with co-workers, God's Word gives us power! As we deal with our Self, God's Word gives us power! The next time you look at your Bible, look at it as your power. Open it, read it, and be empowered! Boring it is not!

The Master's Plan

Firstborn has made up his mind, and has decided to join the military. I wanted him to finish college and get his degree, yet I remind myself that what I want for his life probably doesn't line up with God's plan for his life. As a mother, I sometimes want to be my sons' God and plan their life for them. Mama knows best, right? Well, not all the time. I know my role is to nurture and guide my sons to the Master Planner, but I sometimes jump out of my lane and into the Master's lane. As Firstborn asked question after question about my Navy experiences, I was hoping he'd choose the Navy, but I ended our conversation by telling him to pray about which branch he chooses to join. *Dear God, please let him join the Navy.*

It's difficult to watch our children grow up and make their own choices, but a mother's role isn't to protect our children *from* life, but to prepare them *for* life. I'm so thankful Firstborn knows His Heavenly Father for himself and understands the power of prayer, so I need to trust my training and let him go. *Dear God, please cover my baby*. I also jumped into my selfish mode and thought about my teenage roommate leaving me in the apartment by myself. *Lord, why now? I need him!* Life is a path of unexpected turns and events. Life never happens the way we plan, but thank God for Jesus! God knew our journey before we were formed in our mother's womb. He knew the journey of our children before they were formed in our womb. Thank God the Master Planner is our keeper, our guide, and our comforter. Thank God He knows what's best! The Master's plan doesn't always look good to mama, but it always works for our good.

Look!

One weekend while Secondborn and I traveled to Alabama to see my parents, I noticed the autumn trees lining the highway. I pointed the beauty out to Secondborn. I didn't want him to miss what I was seeing. I wanted him to take notice of the changing of colors and seasons in the beautiful trees. I related awareness of the trees to awareness of life. We can continue to drive by the trees and focus on our destination, but we'll miss the beauty the trees behold. Life is the same. I can continue focusing on my goals, dreams, and desires and miss the beauty of the journey of my life. My journey is the changing seasons of life, and the lessons and beauty they hold. Even today as I drive within my city, I should focus more on my journey rather than my destination. Most of the time, I'm rushed, so beauty isn't on my mind, but getting where I have to go is; therefore, I miss my journey. If I'm not careful, I'll miss the journey of life by rushing to always meet the demands of others or feeling like my life is not fulfilled. It's so easy to fill life with meaningless events. Just because our days are full doesn't mean our life is fulfilled. Life is fulfilled when we fill it with the One who created it! He is the source of our joy and fulfillment – nothing and nobody else can fulfill us like He can. I hear older people say all the time, "Life passed me by." This is scary; I don't want life to pass me by. Life is like a vapor – here one minute and gone the next. Let's embrace this quickly-disappearing vapor called life. Let's slow down and look at life happening all around us. Let's recognize the journey – not the destination.

Life Itself

One Sunday afternoon, I felt the need to leave my laptop and take a walk. It had been a while since I took a walk just to be walking, and the walk was more than refreshing. Being outside reminded me of how much I love the outdoors. I always pictured myself living on a ranch with horses, in a ranch-style home with rocking chairs on the porch, and being able to walk outside and ride my horse for hours. Well, I didn't have a horse to ride, but my two feet took me around the trail several times. I felt like a different person. I probably had a smile on my face the entire time as I inhaled the fresh air, felt the sun warming my skin, and listened to the birds around me sing. Life is a gift – a blessing - a treasure that gets buried under the life we create around it. As we're busy raising children and grandchildren, serving our spouse, building a career, enlarging our ministry, and accumulating more stuff, the simple joy of life itself creeps by. It's easy to get lost in life by not taking time to "smell the roses." I don't want to work so hard that I don't have time to enjoy the beauty of life itself. Although I love to write, sometimes I need to look up over my laptop and realize life is passing by. I don't want my labor to consume my life. When I'm on my deathbed, I don't think I'll say, "Dang, I wish I had written one more book." It's time to stop to smell the roses, and simply enjoy life itself.

I Shall Not Want

The Lord is my shepherd I shall lack nothing. I have to repeat this in my head when I find myself focusing on what I need or what I want. Lack of income, lack of gas, lack of clothes, lack of creativity, lack of companionship, lack of health, lack of time or lack of time alone. The lack of anything can sneak up and cause worry and doubt in the mind, which causes our focus to leave the Provider. If I can be real, the only thing we *really* lack, as children of God, is the ability to realize we don't have to lack anything! We make a choice to be without because the Lord is our Shepherd and we shall lack for NO THING! No matter how impossible the situation appears or what we might need, God will *always* make a way. Hasn't He always? He *always* delivers. He *always* provides! He is our supply and our supplier. Even when we place ourselves in a situation of lack by overspending or mismanaging our money, He *still* shows mercy and provides! If this isn't enough to make you shout, I don't know what will. We either believe in God or we don't. Let's not do like our children sometimes do. They'll say they're hungry, but the refrigerator is full of food. They'll say they're bored and they have every toy and electronic device possible. My mother used to say we were crying because we were hungry with a loaf of bread under our arm. Funny, but true! We serve a King and we are the King's children – we shall lack for NO THING for He has everything we need and want.

Swing the Bat

Inspired by Terrell Washington, AL

I received an unexpected phone call last night from a dear friend I've known since junior high school. I hadn't heard from him in a while, so we caught up on the happenings of life. After all the small talk, my friend said life was similar to being up to bat in a baseball game - when the ball comes we'd better swing. I was so impressed with the analogy shared; I had to add my own spin to it – no pun intended. Standing outside the batter's box, I take a few practice swings. When I feel I'm ready, I step into the box in my best batter's stance. The pitcher, an opposing team member with a mission to strike me out, could actually be a close friend, family member, or co-worker. The ball represents life and the many things life throws our way.

Because baseball is my favorite sport, I'm familiar with a few different pitches. The ball can come across home plate high, low, inside, a change-up, slider, splitter, or even a curve ball, but in order to stay in the game, we need to swing the bat. Striking out is not an option, but it *may* happen. I can only do my best; so I must keep my eye on the ball and swing the bat. I'm not trying to hit the ball out of the park; my goal is to just hit the ball. There is no telling what type of ball is coming across home plate, but when it comes, swing the bat! We know it's coming, so swing! What happens after we swing is out of our control, all we can do is focus and swing - watch and pray - trust and believe. So, with that being said, are you ready to swing your bat? If not, find your batter's stance (prayer position), and get ready because the ball is coming. Swing the bat!

Your Story

My favorite part of writing is helping others write. I especially enjoy watching memoirs come together from a few shared stories. So many think they don't have a story to tell, but *everyone* has a story. The occurrences and events that happen in our life, and how they amazingly mold us to be the women we were created to be, is a story! Our circumstances continually build our character – that's a story. Our storms strengthen us – that's a story. Our marriages and relationships with our children reveal who we really are – now, that's a story! I enjoy experiencing how a complete stranger comes into my life wanting help with their memoir, and I slowly become a part of their life. I get consumed with their struggles, triumphs, tests and trials, and find a way to word them, so others can benefit from them. This morning, I thought of someone's life story that I definitely benefit from. It was written a long time ago, but each time I pick up their book, I benefit from it. Their story gives me hope, joy, and most of all, peace! Their story is one that I have to tell others about because it's too good to keep to myself. Their story never gets old, and I can read it every day, and get refreshed and renewed. You know this person's life story also. Yep, it's our Heavenly Father's story. Doesn't He have a great story? This is definitely one story that I want to be consumed with and become a part of. His story appears to have ended in death, yet He continues to live and He gives us life! So, as we live day by day creating our own life story, let's remember the one story that is the beginning and the ending of all stories – His Story.

Mountain Climbing

Last night before going to bed, I stood in the middle of my living room and prayed. An old gospel song came to mind, and I sang just a few words of it over, and over again. They were, *Lord, don't move my mountain, but give me the strength to climb.* I've got a big mountain in front of me right now and as much as I would love God to miraculously move it to the side or allow me to walk around it, I know it's here for me to climb. Auuuugh! Why now, Lord? Through my carnal eyes, this mountain is such an inconvenience. It could not have come at a more inconvenient time, but I know from past mountains that my inconvenience is definitely God's perfect timing. In the past, I've looked at my mountains as distractions or obstacles, but previous climbs taught me this mountain is *only* here to strengthen me. It doesn't matter what the mountain is made of or how it got here, what matters is that I get to the top.

Believe it or not, God prepared me for this mountain. I saw it coming, but I didn't think it would be so enormous; it's overwhelming, but you know what? It doesn't matter how big the mountain appears, my God is bigger! It looks like a hard climb, but my God told me I was more than a conqueror. It looks scary, but God didn't give me the spirit of fear, but of power, love, and a sound mind! He told me I could do all things through Him. Are you staring at any mountains? I know it's tiring and frustrating, but we've climbed mountains before. On our climb, let's remember to look *up* all the way to the top because that's where our strength is coming from. Okay, Lord...don't move our mountain, but give us the strength to climb!

Cozy

It may sound lazy, but when I opened my eyes this morning, I went right into prayer and meditation mode – I didn't even get out of bed. I curled up in my sheets and smiled as I spent time in my Heavenly Father's presence. The love God has for me makes me smile, and that's just what I did as I basked in His presence in my warm bed. I knew I'd have to get up sooner or later because life was calling.

Life isn't rolled up in my sheets praying and meditating. Life is when I put my feet on the floor and get ready for battle. Life isn't singing praises to God in the shower, but life is dealing with difficult people and the issues of the day. Life isn't wrapped up in the coziness of my apartment with my sister's colorful art covering every wall, but life is the sum of the people I come in contact with throughout the day and how I interact with them. Life is the sum of choices I'll make today. Life is a collection of the thoughts and moods I choose to entertain.

One good thing about life outside of the coziness of my palace of peace is that I can still be in the presence of God when I walk out into the reality of life. I can still bask in His presence and smile when I think of His goodness. I can still pray without ceasing and meditate on His word. No it's not easy, and we all have to deal with the noises of life whether they're inside or outside of the home. Where's the peace? The peace is in our heart, in our mind, and in that secret place, that cozy place, where we mentally retreat to, and intimately bask in the presence of our loving God.

Separated

When I first started writing, I was married with children. Now separated, I look back and see how God not only disconnected me from my marriage, but from people and things that hindered me from hearing His voice loud and clear. Before I moved, I had to disconnect the cable, telephone, and of course the water, and electricity. Disconnecting the home phone disconnected me from my prayer partner of twelve years.

I had a Tracfone at the time, but needed to save my minutes for emergency calls, so our 5:30 morning prayers together ceased. Not only did I stop communicating with her, but I wasn't communicating with anyone. Disconnecting cable disconnected me from television and the only other form of communication I had at home – email. The boys still had their gaming system, so they were content. For several weeks, God had my undivided attention. It was just Him and me. I did more meditating (listening) than praying (talking) because I really didn't know what to pray about. I was in a state of....disbelief? Was this really *me* in this situation? Did I really make the decision to walk away? I wasn't doubting my decision, but amazed that I actually found the courage to do it.

Not knowing what was ahead of me, I continued to be quiet. My disconnect actually connected me to God like never before. I had peace – perfect peace in the midst of my situation – my storm. I had courage instead of confusion. I had wisdom instead of worry. I had assurance instead of anxiety. I had a connection in the midst of my disconnection. Although I was separating from a man, I had oneness with my God who assured me He'd always be my Protector, Provider, and my Prince of Peace.

As mothers, we often try to shield our children from the hardships of life. Watching them make mistakes and endure challenges can become a storm for us! The best thing we can do is to ensure our children are prepared for their own storms of life. As we grow spiritually, we want to take our children with us to those higher levels of learning.

Following are words written by the mother of an eleven year old victim of bullying. Ms. Kirk was kind enough to share her pain as a mother. Her daughter, Carys, has written a poem and also agreed to share.

I Saw Red!

Laura Kirk, AL

I have had low self-esteem and insecurities for as long as I can remember, so my goal was to make sure my children didn't have that battle. Then I find out my beautiful, sweet, loving, creative daughter was being bullied at school. When I discovered what was happening I saw RED! Then I found out my daughter was being shunned, ridiculed, and belittled and it had been going on for approximately three years. To make matters worse it was a Christian school, and the teacher's daughter was one of the main bullies. I met with the principal, who then brought my child into the office. My daughter informed her that she felt like she was in hell when she was at school! The principal and staff did nothing to protect my daughter or change the behavior of the bullies, so I took matters into my own hands. I let my daughter know she was strong because instead of becoming a bully herself to try and fit in, she stayed true to who she was a loving heart and kind spirit. Every morning we would say three things we were thankful for, two things we liked about ourselves, and one thing we like about each other. I let her know these girls were nothing in her world and she would not even remember their names in five years. I tried to empower my daughter, Carys, instead of allowing her to be a victim.

THE TRULY FREE

Carys Kirk, AL

Forsake me,
Forsake me,
But you cannot break me.

I am not the trained dog of man,
I am not the circus monkey Tamaran.

I am not the saddled horse,
You cannot decide my heart or mind's course.

Forsake me,
Forsake me,
But you cannot break me.

Any beast or human join me,
Under the starry night or forest tree.
Under the power of God, our king,
Join me so we can truly be free.

Forsake we,
Forsake we,
But you cannot break we, the free.

The moon was made when God said, "Let there be light."
The greater to rule the day, the lesser to govern the night."

So with the sun being the greater and the lesser being the moon,

The sun was placed into the day, and the moon cocooned in the night.

Books by LaVender S Williams

We Snap in Silence

Trash Thoughts

Can I Be Real? Reflections of a Real Housewife

The Struggle: My Life and Legacy (with Bernice Sims)

Resurrecting Life Through Double Life Sentences

www.lavenderwilliams.com
www.momsweb.net

If you'd like to receive LaVender's weekly Monday
Meditations, send an email to momsweb@momsweb.net
with ADD ME in the subject line.

www.candypublishing.net

Candy Publishing is an independent publishing company designed to help aspiring writers put their life in print. We work on-on-one with writers to create eye-catching, one of a kind memorable books. We bring your book to life!

When All Hell Breaks Loose

Editing
Jackie D. Rockwell
www.Awomanofherwords.com

DK1 Promotions
www.dk1pro.com

SmartPR & Consulting, LLC
www.smartprconsulting.wix.com

Cover / Interior Art
Deborah Shedrick
www.dshedrick.com

www.ingramcontent.com/pod-product-compliance
Lightning Source LLC
Chambersburg PA
CBHW051238090426
42742CB00001B/4

9 780692 642900